Journal of a Christian Warrior

Book 1

By

Rev. Warren Houston

Table of Contents

Introduction

Today, I would like to give honor to God, His son Jesus, and the Holy Spirit. I would like to thank anyone who is reading this for reading this. The stories that you are about to read are all true. It is a chronicled account of spiritual encounters that I've had throughout my life. At the time of this writing, I am 62. I am not going to write about every event that occurred. There have been so many events in which I dealt with the Holy Spirit or an angel that it would take many books to fulfill that task. After much prayer and supplication, I chose to write a series of books that I call my journals to cover as much as I can.

There will be one book broken into three sections, creating three sub-books totaling 33 events. Book 1 covers the teen years. Book 2 covers the young adult years, and book 3 brings you to the current. Due to the intensity of some of the content I felt smaller bites were better, as some events can be spiritually challenging. I made sure that there were 33 events I was writing about because the number 33 is very important to me. During the time of my life when I was playing sports, I needed to choose a jersey number. I did not select the number 33. I was presented with the number 33, and that's the number I'm sticking with.

Now, all Christians and many non-Christians are aware of what the number 33 means to us. When I was given the number 33, I did not understand its significance. I had chosen number 22 after my favorite player, who played for the Miami Dolphins and wore number 22. But the Lord has his own ways and means and direction that things should go, and believe me, you're better off following his path because our paths are all crooked and broken.

As for this prologue, I am not going to take a long time about writing anything in this particular place. Those who know me know that I am not a beat-around-the-bush kind of guy, and I like to get to the point. With that said I would like to thank the following persons for their words and encouragement throughout these years.

For anyone that I overlooked, I'm sure you will let me know, and I will somehow make amends. I would like to thank my wife, Deborah, who bore witness to some of these events. My children Harmony and Amaris, who with their encouragement and involvement, managed to end up in these books also. To Crystal, who was as close to the action as you can get. To my mother, who was the first to say, "Ant, you need to start writing this stuff down." When she said this, I was 27, and we had no idea what was left to come. I would like to thank my stepmother and my dad, who also witnessed several things. I would like to thank my sister and my brothers for their words of encouragement. I send out special thanks to Ray, Cal, and Marcos for their words of encouragement and guidance. These three guys called me on the carpet for many things, and trust me when I say I am not an easy guy to call on the carpet. And let me not forget my family, especially Terry, Clem, Clarence, Barry, Howard, Michael, Vincent, Eric, Chris, Weaver, Sarah, Sharie, Dave, Daniell, Jennifer, Olin, Walt, and many others like cousin Virdie, Aunt June, Aunt Gracie, and Aunt Betty. And how can I not mention the Erv, who has been there through thick and thin. There are so many others that I did not name. But even though I cannot mention everyone here, I have not forgotten them, and I will not forget them. May all of you be blessed by the Lord who sits high and looks low that a blessing is spent unto you. Thank you for being there.

And now may the Lord of Hosts, who knows these writings to be true and honest to the best of my recall, bless these writings, those involved, and those who remember in the name of Jesus, we pray amen.

Without further ado, let the Journal be written and the stories be told. I spared no expense.

Entry #1: The Arrival

Jeremiah 1: 5 – 9

5 Before I formed thee in the belly I knew thee; and before thou camest forth out of the womb I sanctified thee, and I ordained thee a prophet unto the nations.

6 Then said I, ah, Lord GOD! behold, I cannot speak: for I am a child.

7 But the LORD said unto me, say not, I am a child: for thou shalt go to all that I shall send thee, and whatsoever I command thee thou shalt speak.

8 Be not afraid of their faces: for I am with thee to deliver thee, saith the LORD.

9 Then the LORD put forth his hand, and

touched my mouth. And the LORD said unto me, Behold, I have put my words in thy mouth.

I chose this passage of Scripture because it best defines my earliest memory of life. Throughout my life I've told those around me that I remember being born. Of all those I've told, only two persons believed me the first time. Those two people were Weaver and Calvin. When I told Weaver, he simply said, "Knowing you that's probably true." When I told Cal, he simply said if you were someone else, I wouldn't believe it, but because it's you I do believe.

All others questioned whether I was actually telling the truth or not. My dad would often ask me, "Do you really think we believe that you remember being born?" I always answer, "Whether you believe it or not, I remember." He would say, "Well, as long as you could talk, you said that you remember being born, so maybe you do believe it but it's hard for me to understand." That being said, I do remember, and that is what this arrival story is about.

When my children were old enough, I asked them if they remembered being born. They both said no and when they were older, they wanted to know why I asked. I explained to them that I remembered being born, and they didn't believe me, especially my oldest child, Harmony. She was quite animated by this claim that I made, and as she got older, she got more animated. It became a game of challenging your father's memory for us.

Then one day, with the use of her iPhone and a computer, she decided to prove me wrong by looking it up on the Internet. Of course, we know that the Internet is full of nothing but truth, right?

So, as she continues her research to prove me wrong, she finally finds the subject that she likes. The title of the subject actually states, "People who claim they remember being born." So, she looks at me and says, "Gotcha! This article will clear this up once and for all!" I reminded her that my faith is not bound or found on the Internet, but that didn't stop her. Amaris, my youngest daughter and self-proclaimed protector, says, "Harmony, if that is what he remembers, then he remembers, why can't you leave this alone?"

Harmony replies, "Because Am. No one remembers being born. It's probably just something that Dad remembers something else, and he thinks it happened while he was being born. No one remembers that."

I stated, "Let her read the research. It may do her some good. After all, it is not going to change anything. I know what I remember. I know what happened. I have no explanation for it myself, but I do know it happened."

As Harmony continued to read this research that she had found all of a sudden, we heard the following: Harmony, "Oh my God!"

We were in the middle of playing spades, the four of us with me and my dad on the old team, as they called us. Just as a note of record, the old team was whipping young behind.

Harmony continued to read without saying anything, but her expression showed bewilderment. Amaris began asking, "What did you find?" Harmony continued to read without responding, but that didn't stop Amaris from asking. Finally, I said, "Am she doesn't want to say that because it proves what I have been saying all along?"

Amaris, "Harmony, what did you find?"

Harmony, "Well, this sounds crazy, but according to this research, there are approximately .5% of the population on Earth who claim they remember being born, and of that percentage, those who repeat the same story over and over tend to share one characteristic."

Amaris, "Well, what is it?"

Harmony was silent as she continued to read, disrupting the flow of the card game. My dad finally said, "Spit it out. What did you find?" After taking a deep breath, Harmony said, "It says of those who remember and could clearly recite over and over the exact details, their only commonality was their IQ was over 180! And they had unusual memory recall. Many of them could remember the specifics of an entire event or day, including such small details as to specific times and items in a room. The research went on to state that there were others who remembered but those with the IQ above 180 had memories far more consistent and clearer than the others."

My dad says, "I guess that settles that. The last time they tested you for your IQ, the score was above 180."

I replied, "Yes, but I was 19 then."

Amaris says, "But it is over that. Now. See Harmony, I told you. Now leave Daddy alone."

The conversation continued, but Harmony was forced to believe that I do have some recollection of being born, whether it's total memory or partial memory. The fact is that I do remember. Now, let's get into the story of the Arrival. I do remember.

The darkness. It was so dark. I couldn't see anything, but I could hear the voices. There were so many voices. And they spoke all the time, not just to me, but to each other and others all around me there were voices. In the presence of others like myself and others unlike me who were different. These others spoke to me. They spoke to everyone. I don't remember what they said, but I do remember hearing constantly, for so long. I have no number that I can put on the length of time that I was in the darkness, but I began to notice that I was moving. Not just moving around, I was moving in a particular direction. I was going forward. Slowly at first, very slow. I could see what appeared to be dots of light, maybe showers of light moving around me as I traveled. At some point I noticed my motion had increased in speed.

I was still moving forward, but it was definitely faster, and the voices were becoming lighter. They weren't as loud as before, but they were still there. There seemed to be more voices from the others than there had been previously. When I say others, I mean those who were not like me.

It was still dark, but I was not afraid. I would say the darkness was friendly; it was what I knew. It was home, if that's what you could call home, and I was aware. I was alive, but I was not here. I don't know where I was, and again, I don't know how long I was there, but the darkness was home.

I liked the darkness. It was familiar to me and the voices kept me company. They knew me and they spoke to me. Strangely enough, I don't remember speaking back to the voices. I just remember being there and knowing I was safe. It felt so good. But now I was moving and again the speed was faster than before. The voices had become less. There seemed to be just a few voices. The voices such as myself I no longer heard. They were gone. They were no longer part of the darkness and there were fewer lights, and I was moving faster. A lot faster.

And then suddenly, my acceleration increased dramatically. The lights now turned into a small spiral, and there was one voice speaking to me, whispering to me. It was still inaudible but clear. The line and the spiral were no longer thin. It had thickened to what I would say is a medium-sized line in the spiral, but it was spinning fast. The spiral now nearly took up all of the darkness. The one voice was still there, but the darkness was disappearing. The spiral had grown so thick, it was now most of all I could see. There was very little darkness left. In case I didn't mention it, the spiral was a bright white light. Not intense light. It was more like a guiding light leading me out of the darkness. But I didn't want to go. I remember thinking, "What is that? Where is that going?

And then there was a bright flash! It was so bright. I didn't want to see it. I didn't like this light. This brightness. The comfort of the darkness was gone. This light was not going to leave. Then I heard the voice. The one voice. The last voice. I actually understood what it said this time. It said, "Open your eyes."

I opened my eyes for the first time ever. I did not know I had eyes but apparently, I did. As my vision came into focus, I saw a man above me. He was a Caucasian male. He had on a white cap, white gloves, and a long white coat. He looked to be pulling on the gloves. He was huge. I'm not sure I knew what huge was at the time, but he was huge. He glanced down. He looked startled and he said to someone I could not see, "I think he's looking at me." He moved away, and I watched him go intently because without the darkness, he was all I had seen.

I wanted the darkness, it was home. I don't know what this is, but it is not the darkness; it is not home. Then a female walked by. Because she was moving, I could not make out full features, but I knew she was a female. She looked down at me and said, "He is looking at you." She also was wearing a white cap and a white coat, but she had a mask on. I could not see her face. She didn't stop. She continued to move on. There are mechanical devices all around the room. I didn't know what they did. I know what they are now. I could describe them, but it is irrelevant. I have arrived. I wanted the darkness, but it was gone just like the voices, and the voice, they were all gone. I was alone in the light. I really just wanted the darkness. Then I heard the voice say, "Sleep." So, I slept. I have arrived.

Entry #2: Grandmas Touch

As I write this, I wonder how important this event was as far as the journal is concerned. Eventually, I surmised that it was important because it was the first full memory that I had. When I say full, I mean the complete day that I remember. I remember a lot of things quite vividly, but this day especially.

My personal belief is that it marks the beginning of my full self-aware memory recall. My recollection of this day to me is amazing. I remember things such as the smell of the room, the sounds in the room, the temperature of the day, what I ate, and seeing people not realizing who they were. Needless to say, I'm not going to go through all that. I'm focusing here on the fact that I discovered for the first time I could remember the entirety of what was taught in those few years. More specifically, I remember, remembering and this is how it happened.

Psalms 103

17 But the mercy of the LORD is from everlasting to everlasting upon them that fear him, and his righteousness unto children's children;

18 To such as keep his covenant, and to those that remember his commandments to do them.

Christmas Day Saturday, December 25, 1965

Time: 5:25 AM

I was awakened by a small pinch. Then, a little harder, another one followed with, "Get up! Mama said get up!"

I opened my eyes to see this young girl standing in front of me. From my perspective, she was huge; of course, I was only three years old, and she was seven. I sat up in the bed and took note of its size. It was big, or you could say I was small either way works. "Get up! It's Christmas!" The young girl said again. She seemed to be a little agitated with me, most likely because I wasn't complying with her commands. What she did not understand was that I didn't even know who she was, and her aggressive nature was not pleasing to me.

As I was trying to acclimate myself to the surroundings, she grabbed me by the arm and shoved me into the living room. I looked around and there was this beautiful tree decorated with lights and shiny stuff with a big star at the top. It was beautiful. There were toys everywhere and presents too. There were people standing in the living room. I didn't recognize any of them, but they seemed to know me. There was music playing something about jingle bell nights on this little radio that was off-white in color. I remember looking at that radio and wondering how that sound was coming out of there. That's amazing. A talking box? I wanted to go over to examine it, but this young girl's hand continued to guide me. I think I would've said something to her about her controlling nature, but I did not know what to say. No words came to mind. I would think that would be common for a three-year-old kid. So, I said the only thing I knew, "She pinched me!" It was more of a whine than an affirmation, and it garnered just as much as a response from the one called Ma. Ma stated, "You keep saying that, but she is your sister. Why would she pinch you."

The sister stated, "I didn't pinch him. Open your toys!" This was a denial and avoidance statement often time used by the guilty sibling to continue their dominance of the younger sibling. I had not learned revenge yet, but when I do, all of this will be rectified.

As I slowly crept by her, she attempted a revenge pinch but failed as I could see it coming. I was not sure what a "sister" was, but having two of them would have been a terrible thing, I thought to myself.

The sister said (after missing her scorpionish death pinch attack), "Merry Christmas. Open something. Those are your toys. Why are you acting so strange? Ma? Why is Ant acting like he don't know nobody." Then, she shoved me further into the room. I was about to respond to her aggressive manner when the red glint of red tinsel hit my eye. I turned to see under the Christmas tree a fire truck. It was red with a white ladder and buttons on top. I dropped to my knees and crawled over to this truck. Just as I picked it up, I saw a robot beside it. It was red also, but it had guns in its chest. Now I began to notice other toys and presents. This Christmas thing was the best ever. I will have to settle up with the Great Pincher at another time.

As the day proceeded and the gifts were opened, we stopped to have breakfast. I had cornflakes. I don't recall if I really liked cornflakes, but that's what I had, and it didn't seem bad. Then Ma announced that we were going to Grandma's and Pop's house. So, we put on our coats, got out the door, and walked approximately 40 yards, and were at Grandma and Pop's house. At Grandma's and Pop's, there were more decorations than there were at Ma's house. The house was bigger, and the decorations were brighter and better and there were more toys.

There was a shove from behind, but this time, it didn't come from the sister. It came from the one called Ma. In case I didn't describe her before, Ma was much larger than the sister, and it seemed that everyone took orders from her. Ma said, "Go in the house, child, and speak to Mama and Pop. As I stepped inside, these two people, known as Grandma and Pop, had the biggest smile on their faces. Bigger than anyone I had seen today. Not that that's saying a lot because all I've seen were these few people. The one called Grandma looked at me and said, "Come and give Grandma a hug." I now understand that from the viewpoint of those standing around, my lack of response meant disobedience, but what it actually meant was I didn't know what a hug was. You see, my memory loss went a lot farther than faces. It included a lack of understanding of words and phrases, places, and simple commands that I had been taught to this day. Needless to say, waking up on Christmas day and no one realizing that you don't know or remember any of the prior teachings is incredibly confusing at any age, especially at three years old. Now, this grandma, who I was looking at, was standing there with her arms out, expecting me to go give her a hug. Even though I didn't remember what a hug was.

This woman called Ma was not feeling this hesitation thing at all, and she stated, "You better go hug Mama and stop acting like you don't know nobody. Mama, he's been acting like this all morning. I don't know what his problem is. He ain't saying much of nothing, and I'm having to tell him everything. I ain't going to keep repeating myself all day. He knows better. Go give Mama a hug like I said!" And with that statement, she shoved me across the room.

Now, my momentum carried me into the room. I saw the toys and the pull to grab them and play with them was strong, but I needed to complete this task about the hug. Clearly, there was something very important about it, more important than the toys.

Even at that young age, I theorized that in order to get to the toys, hugs were going to be necessary. They seemed to be the key to getting to the toys. No hugs, no toys.

So, I continued my approach to Grandma. After all, she did seem familiar. They all seemed familiar. I never felt that I was among strangers. I just did not know anyone's name, yet I knew them. Once I got within about 3 feet of Grandma, she scooped me up. What happened next, I truly have no explanation for, except to say Grandma's touch was the best touch ever. When she grabbed me, a myriad of memories cascaded through my mind so fast, so clear, with such vivid recollection that my mind, my little three-year-old mind, could barely hold itself together. I began to cry. Her touch was so gentle, loving, and warm that crying seemed to be the right thing to do. She said, "There goes my puddin'. See, he's all right. He just needed to see Grandma. See, he knows me. Now go open some presents and play with your toys."

For a few more moments, I continued to hold onto her so tight as to never let go. When I let go, I ran back over to Ma and hugged her because now that I remembered what a hug was, I knew why you gave them out. They are for those who love you. As for my Grandmas' hug, it was different. It was more than a hug. Somehow, someway, her hug contained something more. In her hug, there was an expression of love that, for me at least, transcended time and space.

Now that my memory was in place and my three years of experience on this planet were now fully and completely under my control, I understood that I really didn't know anything other than grandma's hugs were wonderful.

While on a field trip in the 7th grade, in a thrift store in the North Carolina mountains, Blowing Rock, to be precise, while looking through the little knickknacks in one of the side shops along the mountain roads, I saw a little sign that said, "grandma's hugs." I bought it for her, and she loved it. What I liked most about the sign was it told me Grandma's hugs happened to be for more than just me. What a great thing it is that God gave us grandmas and grand pa's.

Entry #3: The Return

Hello, and good day. This is a great day for the third story. This one is different from the others because it involves death. You see, I died as a child, at the age of four years old. It's one of those things that in African-American families they don't talk about. You know what I mean. All families have secrets, and some of those secrets have good reasons, and others are just strange. Like when your family tells you to not ask Uncle Stan to help you with your homework. They never say Uncle Stan can't read or if Aunt Sue cooks don't eat it. They don't explain that Aunt Sue doesn't wash her food so the grit you find in the green beans is real grit. Somehow it manages to be different in all families. In my case, the event happened suddenly, within 72 hours, and everyone there was told not to speak about it, especially to me.

This event was a mystery to me until I was 11 years old. I was in the sixth grade when I contracted the measles. Who knew this was going to happen? I had been vaccinated. They checked my records. And yet, I still got the measles. I was the only one in the sixth grade who got the measles. I did not know until recently that they actually closed the school down while they checked records and checked for an outbreak of measles.

Because of my illness I was staying with my grandmother Long. While preparing my lunch, she said to me, "I know you are sick and you feel bad, but you will get over this. This is nothing like what you went through before. We lost you for a little while." That statement made me curious. Lost me where? I don't remember being lost anywhere, at any time, by anyone. So, I said, "Lost me where? Was I at the store?"

She said, "No, not that kind of lost."

I said, "I'm confused. Is there another kind of 'lost'?"

She said, "Well, yes." There was a moment of silence, as if she were gathering her thoughts. This is most likely because this was the first time someone had told me anything like this. She continued to work on my bologna sandwich as she spoke.

She said, "When you were a little boy, you got sick. Very sick. Nobody knew what was wrong with you."

I said, "Y'all took me to the doctor and he fixed it."

She said, "Yes, we took you to the doctor, but he couldn't fix it. The doctors didn't know what was wrong, so the doctor took you to the hospital, and they didn't know what was wrong either."

I said, "So I got lost at the hospital?"

My grandmother didn't say anything. She gave me my sandwich and went and sat in the living room where she continued to watch a soap opera. I finished eating and started playing with toys in the living room. My grandmother watched her soap operas in her room, which was adjacent to the living room. All of us kids knew interrupting a soap opera had a penalty next to death. I was curious but not stupid; also, being lost couldn't be that bad. After all, I'm here so somebody found me.

After a little while, I don't know how long it was. I had become engrossed in a battle of G.I. Joe versus the green army men. My grandmother came back into the living room and sat down on the couch. Then she continued the story.

She said, "After being in the hospital for that day, they sent you home. Everybody was praying for you to get well but it didn't work. It was the night after they sent you home that we lost you."

I continued to play with my toys because even though I was lost, I was here now, so it couldn't have been so bad. I believe that as my grandmother was speaking, she was watching for my reaction, and when she saw that I was not reacting, she realized that I did not think this was serious, but it was. That's when she hit me with the bombshell.

She said, "You died as a child."

When she said this G.I. Joe had one of the Army men in a headlock. I stopped, and I looked at her in full bewilderment. I didn't know what to say. What do you say when you're 11 years old, and someone tells you that you died at age 4? If they gave a class on how a child should react to this kind of news, I missed it. My grandmother looked at me and smiled and laughed a little at my reaction. She now knew she had my full attention as G.I. Joe and the Colonel fell to the floor.

She said, "That's right. We lost you that day. You died!"

I still said nothing. This was shocking news. How did I die, but now I'm here? As I understand, this was not possible. However, the fact that I was here stated otherwise.

I said, "I died?"

She said, "Yes, but you came back."

As I sat there still in a state of shock, she continued.

"You used to tell me this wonderful story about being in a garden. You said it was so beautiful... That it was full of butterflies, birds, and fish. You used to tell me about running around and playing in this garden, and you were having so much fun. You used to talk about the big man in the garden that glowed."

I said, "Yes, I remember. He did glow."

She smiled remembering the story and she continued:

"You said he made you come back. That you weren't wanting to come back."

I said, "I know. He made me come back."

She said, "I know. You said you were not going to tell anybody else the story anymore because no one believed you. I just want to let you know that that's not true. We believed you but we just didn't know what to say. I told you not to tell anybody because you died and went to heaven. We don't know why, but you did. What happened to you there changed you as a little boy. When you came back, you were different. It was almost as if you were no longer a little boy. I told you not to tell anyone your story anymore because there are those who would pick on you and not believe you. But I loved to hear you tell the story. It was always the same and it always made me feel so good to know what waits for us all."

And on that day, I was brought up to speed. Before that, I had thought that memory was from either a TV show or a dream. But it seemed too real to be a dream and most of the TV shows were in black and white, at least on our TV. Now I needed answers. So, I asked my sister, brothers, mother, father, other grandparents, and aunts and uncles about this. Most of them didn't want to say anything for whatever reason, but there were two of them that gave very good descriptions with lots of detailed information, and they were my mother and my oldest brother Jeff. Jeff, being the oldest child, considered himself the family protector, and he was. He would go out of his way to get you out of harm's way. Their version of what happened filled in the gaps. Before I go into that level of detail, first let me just say these were the replies from the others that I asked.

Rosalind (sister): I don't really remember much about it other than you got sick and was burning up with a fever, and they said you were going to die. Everybody was praying and sad. That's all we could do.

Grayling (second oldest brother): I don't talk about it. You got sick and were dying for no reason. I was mad. Nobody could do anything. I didn't believe that. For a long time, I thought they just let it happen but then after you came back, the story you told let me know that this is all for a reason. I don't know what the purpose was but I knew it was God.

Aunt June: Anthony, don't ask me no questions about that. All I know is that it happened and I'm glad it's over and ended like it did.

My dad: I don't know what happened. You got sick and they said they couldn't help. They said you were going to die and there was nothing they could do. They even took you to the white folks' hospital. They don't do that for black folk. But the doctor got it done for you so I guess they were telling the truth as far as trying their best. I was mad. It didn't seem fair. You were outside playing then all of a sudden, you're sick and dying? That doesn't make sense, but it happened. Anyway, whatever happened, you didn't act or play like the little boys who played with you anymore. You ran and played like a little boy but you played different. You seemed to be more watchful, attentive, and mindful of what was going on. It was like you were always thinking.

Jeff: you got sick; I was trying to figure out why. There had to be a reason. The only symptom you had was the fever. You were burning up! It didn't make sense. I looked up illnesses and all kinds of stuff... there was nothing there. Just fever. You started out at 102 and went up to 105 in three days with no other symptoms. My brother was dying, and I could do nothing about it... that's not happening. The one thing I could do was pray. I told God that I was not going to let you die. And I meant that! On the day you died, I was sitting right beside you. I was reading the Bible to you. I have made up my mind since this is the day that they said that you would either live or die and that I was going to sit by your side and make sure that you are not going to die. Not on my watch. But you know what? As I was reading the 16th Psalm, I fell asleep. I had looked at the clock it was about 3 am in the morning. And I fell asleep on the job. I woke up around 4 o'clock, and you were gone. You weren't breathing. I touched you, and you were cold as steel. Your skin was dark, and you were so cold. I didn't know what to do, so I grabbed you and started shaking you to wake you up. I started calling your name, but you wouldn't wake up. Then Ma and them came into the room. They were just standing and watching me. I was still shaking you, calling your name. That went on for about five minutes or so. At some point, Ma grabbed my arm and said, "Jeff stop!" I snatched away from her and said, "No! I'm not going to let him die!" I laid you down and kept calling your name and I kept getting closer to your face as I was calling you. I could hear them crying… everybody crying… but I wouldn't stop. I couldn't stop. I kept getting closer to your face until my nose touched yours. Your nose was cold, but I kept calling, and I was crying, and then you took a deep breath- A deep inhale and opened your eyes!

I turned to Ma and shouted, "He's alive! Ma! He's alive!" And what did you do? You looked around at everybody and said, "I'm hungry." You got out of bed like nothing ever happened. You walked to the kitchen and sat down waiting for a bowl of cereal. Everybody was in shock. Ma told Rozie to fix you a bowl of cereal. Grandma Long said, "Don't nobody say nothing about this to nobody." That's why nobody would say anything to you about this when you kept bringing it up.

My Grandfather (Pop) and Grandma Houston:

Pop said, "There's not much to talk about. You got sick, something happened, and that's about all we know. This is the Lord's work. The rest of us need to just leave it alone."

Grandma Houston: my grandmother was a very sensitive person. She never spoke about it because when I asked her, she would just start crying, so I didn't ask her.

Ma: It always took my mom a little while to say something about this. She seemed to always start off by saying, "Well, there was a lot going on. You had this fever and we couldn't break it. We tried all kinds of stuff. We gave you aspirin and castor oil, and nothing seemed to work. Things were just happening so fast. There just didn't seem to be enough time to do anything.

You were outside playing and you came in and said you didn't feel good. I touched your forehead, and you were burning up. You weren't sick before you went outside. I did not know what to think. That's when we gave you some aspirin and, a few hours later, a dose of castor oil, but that didn't do anything. So, the next morning we called Dr. C and he told us to bring you up there. I used Pop's car to take you up there. Dr. C looked at you for a little while. Then he told me we need to get you to the hospital fast. I thought we were going to the hospital in Mooresville because, you know, that's where they took black folk. But Dr. C said He needed to take you to Charlotte Memorial. I didn't think that was going to work because of time (1966). It didn't matter how sick we were. They were not going to let us into a white hospital. But Dr C. said that it was okay and he would make it work. He called an ambulance, and we followed them down to Charlotte Memorial Hospital. I remember he had talked to a lot of people at first but they finally took you in. I really don't remember what room we went in. Seems like it was some kind of side room, but there were other doctors in there along with Dr. C.

Dr. C said they were going to pack you and ice to try to slow the fever. I set out in the hallway with June. I don't remember much about what went on. I know they kept you overnight and the next day when we went down there, Dr. C told me that they were going to send you home. He said they couldn't break the fever and was now at 105. They put you back in the ambulance and brought you home. Dr. C came with them. He left and came back later. That's when he said, "We can't break the fever. He's burning up. He would either live or die tonight. All we can do is pray."

That's about all I remember until I heard Jeff yelling your name. He set up beside you all night reading the Bible. He said he was not going to let you die and God was going to help him. I didn't say nothing to him. When I went to bed that night he was still sitting and reading.

Sometime over in the morning, I heard Jeff yelling your name so I got up. He was shaking you or holding you or something like that and yelling your name. He kept doing that for a while. I finally tried to stop him. He jerked away from me. He was still yelling. I didn't know what to do so I let him yell. I don't know how long I stood there watching him. But then all of a sudden, he turned around and hollered, "He's alive! He woke up!"

When Jeff moved, you were just sitting up looking like nothing ever happened. You got out of bed, went to the kitchen, and said, "I'm hungry." Everybody was stunned. It was like you were never sick at all. I don't remember a whole lot more about that day. But I do remember that when we got to Mother's she told everybody not to say nothing about this to anybody. I do remember that.

Ok, I'm done with the interviews. That was pretty much everyone who was willing to say something. My Aunts (Grandmother's sisters) occasionally would refer to me as "special little boy." Of course, most of my cousins my age would hear that and say I was being called that because I was stupid and make a joke out of it. I was not picked on too much because I was bigger than most of the kids my age. There was this one day at my Aunt Lilly's house when we (kids) were playing outside, and the term "special boy" came up. My Aunt Lilly came outside on the porch and said, "Stop all that picking! You know better! Ya'll better be careful! That boy is protected by God so, you better stop before you get yourself in trouble!" Aunt Lilly did not like for anyone to pick on anyone. She kept foster kids with disabilities, so she had no tolerance for bullies. We toned it down. Aunt Lilly wouldn't hit you, but she would command your mother to do it without hesitation! That command never happened to me just so ya'll know.

Now, from what I remember. It was a cold November day. Thanksgiving had just happened, but it was not so far past for Christmas lights to be put up. We were one of those families who went all out for Christmas decorations. I remember cars coming by and looking at the houses and how lit up they were. We weren't the only ones. The entire road would dress up for Christmas. It was so much light that you didn't need lights on the inside of the house. But as I said, there were no lights up yet.

My cousin Vincent and I were in the front yard playing with a little plastic bronze football that everyone had seen before. Yes, they still sell them. It was cold and getting near dark, but the sun had not gone down. We both wore hoodies and jeans. My hoodie was grey with the little football emblem on it, and Vincent's was brown.

It was breezy that day. It was Wednesday. I know this because this event lasted for three days and it was Saturday morning when it ended. There was a cold wind that blew by us and I pitched the ball to Vincent. For a brief instant after I pitched the ball there was a man standing beside him. The man was dressed in a black suit with a long coat, white shirt, and a big-brimmed black hat. He looked strange because his face was whiter than his shirt. Chalky white. I stopped as he pitched the ball back but the image was gone. Less than a second went by. A glimpse of a shadow or the sun playing with the wind to create shadow images I thought to myself.

As I pitched the ball back to Vincent there was another wind that came through. This wind was different. It was much colder than any wind I had felt all day. It was icy and sharp. It didn't seem to pass by like the other winds. Even though I had my hood up, I could feel this wind on the left side of my face. It felt like it was on the inside of the hood, moving against my cheek. I turned my head slightly to get away from the feeling, but it moved suddenly toward the front of my face and thrust into my left nostril. A sharp, cold pain filled the left side of my face and brain. I grabbed my face, and the ball hit me in the chest. For a moment I just stood there holding my face.

Vincent, "Why didn't you catch the ball?"

I wanted to reply but the pain was so intense that I couldn't. The left side of my face was on fire! There was an ice-cold stick feeling in my nose with the tip lodged between the corner of my eye and the bridge of my nose. It seemed to me that it was causing the fire in my brain because the pain was so intense. Vincent picked up the ball.

Vincent said, "You ready?"

He pitched the ball again, and it hit me in the chest again. I turned and started to walk toward the house. Vincent called me, "Ant! Ant! What's wrong? Are you going to play? Ant!"

I kept walking. The pain was so intense that I could not talk. I was clenching my teeth because opening my mouth made my face hurt more. Vincent was following me because, as the older of the two of us, it was his responsibility to make sure no one got hurt. Since it now looked as if I was hurt, he would have to answer so many questions.

I walked into the living room and my mom was sitting on the couch with my younger brother Chavis sitting beside her. Chavis was 2 years old. Our house was only 900 sq. Ft.- A 2-bedroom house with no interior plumbing. We had a pot belly stove in the living room approximately 8 feet from the front door. The kitchen area was to the left of the front door, and both bedrooms were off each side of the pot belly stove. There was an outhouse. These were the conditions for most people in our neighborhood.

I walked over and stood in front of my mother still holding my face:

Ma, "Why aren't you playing?"

Vincent, "I didn't do nothing."

Me, "I don't feel good."

These were the last words that I would say for the rest of the event. Talking caused so much pain that I did not have the strength to do it. After this, all questions went unanswered. My mom touched my forehead with the back of her hand and said, "Oh

Lord, he's burning up." She touched my hoodie and said to my Aunt June, "He's wet! Soaking wet!"

I don't remember laying down but we know that is what happened next. From this point, things were a bunch of images and conversations. The following is what I remember:

Someone giving me castor oil. This stuff was the black family go to in the south. It never worked. Fortunately, due to my illness, I couldn't taste it. It made me sicker and caused me to throw up.

Someone carrying me to my grandfather's car (trust and believe it was not my grandfather most likely Jeff). The same person carried me into Dr. C's office.

Dr. C asking me questions.

Ambulance ride to somewhere.

Voices discussing using ice to address a fever. I didn't know what that meant or who they were talking about.

Waking up in a tub surrounded by ice. I could not feel the cold from the ice. Standing to my right were Dr. C. and 2 other men all dressed in white coats. I heard Dr. C. say, "I am taking him home. I don't want him to die here." I still don't know who they are talking about.

Waking up at home again. I was on the rollaway bed in the living room. Dr. C. was kneeling beside me with his assistant standing over him. I thought it was strange that his assistant was dressed in all black with a big black hat on. He reminded me of the man who was standing beside Vincent when we were outside. I could not see his face but he was a big fella. Dr. C. got up and turned to my mother and said, "Iretha, he will either live or die tonight. He can't go on like this. He is burning up inside, and we can't break this fever. We have tried everything. Now we pray."

I saw a lot of people standing around the bed, most of them strangers. I noticed Dr. C's assistant stayed. I saw Ma and Jeff sitting in the chair beside me with the Bible. I did not hear anyone say anything. I went to sleep, and then there was the bright light, the sound of birds, and the smell of flowers.

When I opened my eyes, I saw the most beautiful place I had ever seen. Granted, I was only four years old, but I had seen pictures. My grandmother subscribed to National Geographic, and we had the World Book Encyclopedia. I don't have the words now or then to describe the beauty of this place. I was in a garden. The smell would tempt you to eat the air, and the colors were so vibrant and diversified that it was incredible.

Everything had a soft white glow. There was a purple, gold, and yellow bush near me on my right. I touched it and the glow seemed to increase. An orange and green tree was on my left. When I reached out to touch it a beautiful blue, yellow, and black butterfly landed on my right hand. I touched it with my left hand and it just fluttered to my left hand. It reminded me of the monarch butterflies from National Geographic. Then this blue and white bird flew in front of me. It hovered but it was not a hummingbird. I reached for it but it moved away. I reached for it again but it would not let me catch it. Then a red and yellow bird with a blue beak dived in and landed on my left arm I tried to touch it but it moved out of range. I looked around and I saw birds and butterflies everywhere. I chased them and they played with me for what seemed like years.

I remember when I first noticed the glowing man. I was chasing and playing with the wildlife so much (or he was not there and I saw him when he wanted to be seen) that I did not see this giant of a man. I noticed him while chasing some butterflies and birds. I came upon this stream. It was so clear that the only way I knew it was a stream was that as I approached it, I noticed these beautiful rainbow-colored fish in it. I jumped over the stream and looked down and saw the fish looking up at me. They were happy and I was too.

As I ran through the garden, I noticed a very large man sitting on a rock watching me. He was absolutely huge (I would guess his size at 15 to 20 feet, but he was sitting, and I was 4, just saying), and he gave off this magnificent glow. I stopped and looked closer. He sat on the rock with his fist on his chin smiling at me. His pose reminded me of "The Thinker artwork." He did not say a thing he just smiled and glowed. I started to realize that it was his glow that illuminated everything and I mean everything. His glow did not pulsate. It was steady and strong. I looked at my hands and arms and I was glowing. His glow covered me too. It felt so good. So, warm and strong.

He was wearing a long white robe with a hood. He was not a white man, a black man, or any man of Earth. He was a glowing man and his beauty was unparalleled. He just smiled, so I went back to the business of playing; after all, that is what kids do best. I have been asked if I was naked while in this garden and the answer is yes, I was. I don't see the importance of that question but that is the answer.

I ran and played to my heart's content. Then he spoke. The glowing man spoke and it sounded like a mountain had moved but it was not deafening nor scary. It was a kind tone but definitely a powerful one.

Glowing man, "You have to leave. You have to go back."

I thought about that for a second and said, "Nope. I'm not going back."

I glanced at him to see what he was going to do. Was he going to come after me? After all, I was a child. We don't get to tell grown-ups what to do especially glowing ones.

He just sat there and continued to smile and watch me play. After a while (I don't know how long. Time seemed to work differently there) he spoke again:

Glowing Man, "You have to go home. You have things to do."

Me, "Nope, I'm staying here. I'm not going back."

He just continued to smile, and I started to play

again. What I didn't realize was that this was not a request. As I continued to play, I first noticed the birds and butterflies fade away, so I stopped running. I looked around and noticed the trees and bushes were gone. Soon, everything was gone, and I was standing in a glowing empty area.

Off in the distance, I heard someone calling my name over and over. It was Jeff, but he was so far away. His voice got louder and louder, and the glow got fainter and fainter until he was so loud that I opened my eyes. His face was so close to me that I could not see anything but him. His nose was touching my nose. I'm thinking, "What is he doing?" He turns and says, "He's alive!" I am thinking, "Who is he talking about?" I can still remember the kitchen light shining over Jeff's right shoulder.

I sat up and saw Ma, Rozie, Gray, and Aunt June all standing around in the living room. I felt incredibly hungry, so I got out of bed, went to the table, and said, "I'm hungry." Rozie normally fixes my cereal, but she doesn't move.

Ma, "Roz fix him his cereal."

I later found out from both Jeff and my mom that Dr. C. didn't have an assistant and his nurse is a female. So, this was my first encounter with this man dressed in black but it would not be my last. At least I had my marching orders: "I have things to do." Let the things begin! And no, I do not know what these things are. God will reveal that as time marches on. Also, understand the references and descriptions are from me as an adult, not as a child.

Entry #4: You are My Warrior

Hello again. That last story was a hum-dinger. Dying and not knowing you're dying is an interesting concept. I am not going to expound upon it except to say there are at least two versions of every story, and then there is the truth. I promise you this next story is not nearly as intense, but it is every bit as factual and necessary for the journey. It's also funny.

It was a spring day in the year 1972. I was in the fifth grade, leading a carefree child's life. As I remember, it was March. It was Sunday, and I remember that because we had returned from church and changed out of our Sunday go-to-meeting clothes.

My mom had cooked before we went to church so as to lessen the load when we got home. Everyone had gone to their separate corners and were doing their own thing. Me, I decided to have a war. G.I. Joe, with the fuzzy beard and General Custer, had decided to invade the little green army men and the bottle cap tanks; a Lego/domino fortress protected them (it was a custom-made job by yours truly). I know most of you have never heard of this but if you don't have the complete set of anything, improvising is a must.

G. I. Joe and Custer were both 12 inches tall and sturdy. They were making great headway against the smaller opponents. I had to add some dinosaurs to assist the little guys. My battle continued until I heard a familiar voice say, "Come outside."

I knew this was the voice that guided me here. So, without hesitation, I got up and went outside on the porch. As I walked through the living room, I saw my sister Roz watching TV and my mom doing the dishes. Roz saw me going to the door and asked me where I was going. I said outside on the porch. She didn't say anything else. At our house, for anyone under the age of 12, there was a guaranteed door check every time.

I went on the porch as instructed and waited. It was only a few moments before The Voice began to speak to me.

The Voice, "You are mine! I am with you!"

I replied, "Yes, I am yours!"

The Voice, "You are mine! I will guide you!"

Me, "Yes, I am yours!"

The Voice, "You are mine! You shall follow my instruction!"

Me, "I will follow!"

The Voice, "You are my warrior! You will fight for me!"

Me, "Yes, I will fight for you!"

The Voice, "You are my warrior! I have chosen you! You will fight for me! You are mine! You are my warrior! You will follow my instruction."

This seemed to go on for a long time. I started to feel as if I was lifted off the ground. I could feel the wind blowing hard, but it was a windy day. It did not change the feeling that I was no longer on the porch. I felt so light that I believed I was going to be swept away by the wind. I had closed my eyes and spread my arms, not as if to fly but to float. I opened my eyes, and lo and behold, I was still on the porch. But it felt good. The sensation of being weightless was indescribably relaxing. Alas, I was not floating. I was firmly planted on the ground. In all honesty, that was no surprise, but it would've been cool to have been floating. I understand now that I was "caught up in the spirit," and that's what the floating feeling was. For those who have ears, let them hear (not everyone will understand this).

I was brought further back into reality when I heard Roz's voice at the door behind me. She heard me talking and came to the door to see who I was talking to. When she saw me standing with my arms spread wide and talking to no one, she became curious and asked, "What are you doing?"

Me, "Talking to God."

Roz, "You're doing what?"

Me, "Talking to God."

After hearing that the second time, Roz turned to my mom in the kitchen and said, "Ma, Ant done gone crazy! He's out here, standing on the porch, saying he's talking to God. He's done gone crazy!" My mom came to the door with the dishtowel in her hands. I could feel her watching me, but I could not move. The Voice was still speaking. Oddly enough, The Voice will not stop speaking just because someone showed up or started speaking. This is currently the same situation. When the Holy Spirit speaks, he doesn't stop because somebody else is speaking or present. He will talk right over the top of you as if you were not there.

As my mom stood there analyzing the situation, she finally asked me what I was doing. I answered, "I am talking to God." She paused for a moment, and she said to my sister, "Leave him alone," and she walked away. I think my sister was stunned that more wasn't said, but she walked away also.

The Voice continued to talk for quite a while longer. There was a lot more. The Voice said many things, but I didn't understand most of them. I believe this continued for about 30 minutes or less. What I didn't realize was that passersby saw me standing on the porch, too. That led to a totally new set of questions that my peers will ask me on the way to school on Monday.

When the Voice grew silent, I went back in the house. I went into the kitchen to get some Kool-Aid, and I heard my mother speaking with my grandmother on the phone about me standing outside, claiming that I was talking to God.

Ma, "Mama, I don't know what to think. You know he's been through a lot, and I guess he really could be talking to God, but what if it's not real? I mean, what do you do? What do you say?"

I kind a felt sorry for my mom at that time. What do you do? What do you say? You have a child who has returned from a visit to the afterlife and now is claiming that God is talking to him? Although I was that child, I am glad that I was not that parent. Being a parent is hard enough without something like this throwing you off balance, along with the difficulty of raising a child normally. In my personal opinion, I believe the number one problem on this planet is poor parenting. No one gets it all right, but getting it all wrong exacerbates the situation. I'm not going to go down that road right now, but it is definitely a topic for discussion at another time.

Monday on the way to school. I didn't think what I had done was strange. But others did. On the bus ride to school, one of my cousins asked what I was doing on the porch.

Harry, "Ant, what were you doing on the porch yesterday?"

Me, "What do you mean?"

Harry, "I saw you standing on the porch with your arms stretched out. You looked like you were trying to fly. What were you doing? Were you trying to fly?"

There were a few others who were laughing, and I was laughing too, because I thought it was funny that they didn't know what I was doing. How could they know? This was a good question, so I answered it.

Me, "I was talking to God."

Harry, "You were doing what?"

Me, "I was talking to God."

The laughing faded away, and everyone turned away from me and started talking about different things. DJ, who was sitting in the seat behind me, tapped me on my shoulder and said, "You were talking to God for real?" I answered, "Yes. Doesn't everybody talk to God? Don't you talk to Him when you pray?" DJ, "Yeah, but He don't answer me back like He answers you."

Me, "He will. He answers everybody at some time."

DJ, "Yeah, but He answers you a lot."

Me, "I think He answers everybody. They just don't want to say it."

CM, "He don't answer nobody like He answers you."

Me, "How do you know if nobody says it."

DJ, "Nobody says it because it's not happening to them; it's happening to you."

Harry turned around and told us to be quiet and stop talking about it because we didn't know what we were talking about. Harry was one of the few older guys on the bus, and the older guys had control. This control did not come from them, but it came from home. We were instructed to listen to the older guys in public settings. So, we stopped talking about it. As we got closer to school, DJ had an itch that he needed to scratch.

DJ, "Ant, what's it like? (whispering)"

Me, "What is what?"

DJ, "You know… You know what I'm talking about. (whispering)."

Me, "No, I don't. What?"

CM, "Yeah, tell us?"

At this point, one of the older guys, Danny, turned around to us and said, "Shut up! That's enough! Don't say nothing else!"

We all got quiet and shut up. You see, Danny had a history of punching you if you didn't listen. He normally didn't give out warnings, so this was a good thing, but you knew it wouldn't last. Just as we got to the school, DJ figured he would get that last question in.

DJ, "Ant, what's it like? You know what I mean?"

Me, "What are you talking about?"

DJ, "Dying. What's it like?"

Me, "What? Why are you asking me? I don't…

But before I could complete my answer, there was a movement in the line. We were standing in line to get off the bus but someone was coming intensely in our direction. It was Danny! He was moving people out of his way and coming in our direction! The look of determination on his face was all that was necessary to let us know that somebody, if not everybody, was getting punched. He punched DJ on the arm. He turned to punch CM, but CM ducked down into the seat.

Danny, "I told y'all to shut up! But y'all want to act stupid! You know not to ask him about nothing like that. DJ, you are going to make me hurt you cause you keep talking about stuff you don't know nothing about! I'm not going to tell y'all again!" Danny gave me the "don't say nothing stare." If you don't know what that is, then you never had older kids punch (or about to punch you) for not doing what they said. Harry was more diplomatic in his responses, but he would punch you too.

Just for future reference, all punches were checked by parental oversite. This was not a punch-a-kid free-for-all. Punching anyone's child without cause was a very bad thing. You had to always be aware of the consequences and repercussions in the black neighborhood.

Thus, the hierarchy in the black neighborhood, on or off the bus, takes effect. The older boys run the show until you become one of the older boys who has to help run the show. So, Danny shut it down for the day. One thing to remember is that at this point in my life, I still didn't know what had happened. As a reminder, I found out in the sixth grade. This was the fifth grade. There were no more questions about speaking with God or God speaking with us for quite some time.

For me, I felt as if I had just been knighted by God to be his warrior. It made me proud to know that He chose me. Even as a kid, I started telling people I was God's warrior. I didn't really know what it meant, and neither did they. People would look at me and smile and say, "Oh, that's nice." I didn't know what it meant either but it did sound good to me. But there were those that were very concerned: demons. They took notice, and they were very concerned. Very, very concerned.

Entry #5: A Walking Spirit

The last event was somewhat intense, especially for an 11-year-old. It's not easy trying to tell your friends that you've been having conversations with God. You get funny looks, whisperings, and a few name-calling. Being in a black neighborhood kind of gives you a little leeway because if you actually are talking to God and you are being belittled because of it, there can be consequences and repercussions from the fact that you are attacking someone who God is working with.

I guess that helped some, but I really didn't give it any thought because it happened all the time. Now, when I say all the time, I don't mean being called out to the porch was a visible option that happened every day because it was not. When I say all the time, I mean throughout the day. The Lord would always have something to say, and very often, it had nothing to do with what you were doing. It was just simply him communicating with you. And it wasn't like when you woke in the morning that he said good morning. At least for me, it didn't work like that.

The next event happened on July 5, 1974. By now, I had heard tales of unseen things making noise. Noises such as wailing, whispers, screams even speech that was mostly inaudible and was not heard by everyone but only the select few who could hear it. I remember my grandmother Long would say spirits walk through her room. Many of the spirits she spoke of she said she knew or remembered them. But there were those whom she never knew, yet they walked through her house. Interestingly enough, these spirits didn't stay. It was as if they were just passing through. This was always a curiosity to me, and years later, I would find out why I believe the spirits passed through my grandmother's house. The house that we were living in used to be the old Negro schoolhouse.

When my grandmother and grandfather were looking for a place to live, they were given the opportunity to live inside the schoolhouse, which, of course, was no longer being used. At some point, the schoolhouse was moved off of the schoolyard and onto this corner lot where it now rests. I believe that these spirits that were passing through were the spirits of the students who attended the schoolhouse. For me, it explains the high volume of traffic that my grandmother witnessed. She always said she had been given the gift of seeing spirits. She once told me she saw her first spirit when she was seven years old. Thank goodness I didn't get this gift. I have seen spirits during my time but not to that extent. You can count the number of times I have seen spirits on one hand, and I would like to keep it that way.

July 4, 1974. We had a cookout that day. Lots of families attended. We were supposed to go swimming the next day, so a few of my cousins had decided to spend the night. My cousin Vincent and I were sleeping on the rollaway bed. The bed was located in the living room, which was adjacent to the kitchen. This was the largest area in the home, and the home was very small, being 1100 sq. ft. (Ma had added a room for Roz). There were eight people at the house, some sleeping on the floor. Me and Vincent were lucky because we got the rollaway bed. That was only because Eric, one of my older cousins, and Vince's older brother, decided to sleep on the floor.

At approximately 3:00 AM, I was awakened by a noise that seemed to be far and distant from the house. I don't understand why I was awakened by this noise, but I was. The sound was that of something large striking something hard. Akin to a baseball bat striking a telephone pole but with much greater force. The sound seemed distant, but it was moving closer. It seemed to be following the railroad track which we live in front of. I decided that I would go back to sleep and ignore this "sound" that I could not explain. But that didn't work. The sound continued to travel down the railroad track and it was getting louder.

It seemed like there was a rhythmic pattern to it but it was so far away it was hard to say for certain. I started to count the seconds between the sounds. Initially, I could count to 12 before the sound hit something. This went on for about a minute, I would say, and by now, I realized it was getting really close. Then it finally sounded like it was in Huntersville. Still following the train track, but now I could only count to 10 before I heard the sound. What made it more terrifying to me was that it now echoed throughout the night. The sound was very loud and reverberating, and I had no idea what it was or what to do. My last attempt to count was disrupted by the sound being so loud that it seemed as if it was trying to stop me from counting. It now sounded as if it was about ½ mile away.

It was at this point that I began to panic. I didn't know what this thing was or what it wanted. I wanted it to go away but that wasn't happening. So, I started calling for my mom, but that wasn't working. She did not respond. Next, I called for my second oldest brother Gray. He was in the room next door on the floor right beside Eric but neither moved. The sound now seemed to be about a quarter-mile from the house. That last strike was so strong that the walls shook. I could hear the dogs in the neighborhood howling and barking and seemed to be chasing this sound.

I grabbed Vincent and shook him several times. He would not awake. I could not believe this! How can no one hear this but me? Then I heard the sound right outside of the graveyard that we lived nearby. It sounded like it hit the church with such force that the church would fall apart. I knew beyond all shadow of a doubt that our house was next, even though there was a house between us and the church. I jumped back in the bed, grabbed the covers, pulled them over my head, and waited.

I remember being so terrified of this sound. There was no long pause for dramatic effect, it just came. At first, there was a loud stomp in the front yard. The stomp was so heavy that I thought the house was going to be lifted from its foundation. I don't know if that was a footstep or earthquake, but whatever this thing was, it was big and very heavy. Just after that first stomp, the loudest most terrifying sound I've ever heard slammed against the side of the house. A shockwave ran through the house with such volume that it caused my ears to ring. The windows shook as if they were coming out of their frame. The walls shook, and worst of all the bed shook, and it felt as if something was pulling on my covers. I was struggling to hold on, but there was a force that was tugging on the covers, and just like that the cover was snatched off of me! I started screaming no, no, no, no! I covered my head with my hands and tried to hide. My mind raced with all kinds of images and I just knew this thing was here to get me. Then I heard the sound again, but this time it was back on the railroad track.

So, I listened as the sound continued down the railroad track. I wanted to start counting again, but my nerves wouldn't let me. The sound continued on and finally dissipated when it got near North Mecklenburg High School which was 1 mile away (going West for those that want to know.) Once the noise struck the house, I heard it exactly 6 more times, and it was gone! I didn't get the covers because I decided that if I moved, it might come back, so I just lay still with my eyes closed, and I started praying, "Lord, please don't let that thing come back."

Once I saw the sun come up, I shook Vincent and asked if he heard the sound and why he didn't wake up when I was shaking him. He said to me, "I don't know what you're talking about. You never touched me. I didn't hear a sound or anything else, so I don't know what you're talking about"

The morning had come and I was asking everybody in the house about the sound. Eric was the only one who responded with a statement that I deemed reasonable, considering that I was 12. Eric said, "I believe you, but I didn't hear anything. You know how you and grandma hear stuff and see stuff?

That's all I can tell you. At least you're still here this time." Gray said to Eric that that wasn't funny. Eric responded, "I wasn't being funny. I was being real. And I'm not saying nothing else about it because I don't want nothing to happen to me." Eric is four years older than me, and Gray is six years older. Their opinions mattered to me. Especially Eric because he seemed to always have this mannerism about him. He was very funny, but he had a serious side that would flip on, and all of a sudden, he would be like he was the foreshadowing of the Grim Reaper. He could be very foreboding, and he told excellent scary stories.

We had gone swimming Monday at Ramsey Creek and all seemed fine with the world. No one heard the sound but me, which made me weird again. I was having fun, but my nerves were still shot from the morning event. I even watched the news hoping there was information about an earthquake or something in the area. Alas, no such luck. That sound was not produced by any natural occurrence in the area. Experiences like this do not leave you unscathed. It makes you look into dark corners, listening for things that aren't there, seeing movements when nothing's moving. Later on in the day, I decided to share this with some of my cousins, mostly older. I understood that the older cousins seem to be in a protective mode most of the time for the younger cousins. It didn't take much or long to find out which cousins were responsible and which were not. In this case, there were three older cousins I was talking to, telling them what happened. They had no answers but I noticed that one of them was unusually quiet. This was Harry the same cousin who talked to me after the bus incident. I asked him, "What do you think the sound was."

Harry, "I don't know." I noticed Harry was looking at the ground as he spoke.

Me, "So you didn't hear it either?" He just shook his head no. Q (Harry's older brother and one of the wisest persons I ever knew) said, "You better quit talking about it before something else happens to you! Ant, you know strange stuff happens to you, and we're not trying to figure out why but you're gon`na have to quit telling us about the stuff because you creep people out when you say stuff like this." So, we decided to go to the park to shoot some hoops. Their information matters a lot to me because they lived in front of the railroad too, on the same road.

As we were walking, Harry dropped to the back. No one really noticed because we didn't have a marching order—we just walked. Once he got beside me, he grabbed me by my arm and said, "Stop."

Harry, "I heard it!" he whispered.

Me, "You heard it?" Stunningly surprised.

Harry, "Shut up, boy! You're too loud!" I noticed that he was shaking and crying. I had never seen Harry cry before.

Harry, "Yeah, I heard. I heard it hit your house. It was so loud I just knew your house was torn up! It seemed like it stopped when it got to your house, but then it came on up the track. I tried to wake people up but it was like nobody could hear me. I did the same thing that you did. I jumped under the covers when it came close to the house, but it didn't hit our house. It just kept going. I don't know if it was after you, but it sure did sound like it stopped at your house. To me, it seems like something was walking that's why you were able to count the steps. Whatever it was, it was walking down the railroad track but it stopped when it got to your house. It went by us and it did sound like it left at North

Meck." He wiped the tears from his face as he was reasserting his confidence.

Me, "Why didn't you say something?"

Harry, "Are you stupid? I can't say anything about this! Stuff like this don't happen to me, it happens to you, a lot! People will think I'm crazy. When you say stuff like this because it always happens to you! We just listen and move on. If I say it, they will think I'm crazy. I just wanted you to know it was real and don't nobody know what it was, and don't you say nothing about what I just told you, or I will beat your ass."

We never spoke about this again. I did find some comfort in knowing that it wasn't just me and there was someone else who heard this "sound." I think that for Harry this was just the beginning of other things that would happen in his life. I believe spiritual awakenings can happen at any age. For me, it was at birth. For others, it was in the teens, 20s, 30s or even later. I do believe that once you get that spiritual awakening call, its own and cracking! You have been selected and drafted into the only real war that exists. The spiritual war… Heaven's War.

Ephesians 6:12

King James Version

12 For we wrestle not against flesh and blood, but against principalities, against powers, against the rulers of the darkness of this world, against spiritual wickedness in high places.

I don't believe humanity has the capacity to understand these awakenings. I believe these things only come from God and are only to serve his purpose. In this case that I've just explained Harry's confession was to give me assurance that this is real and that the spirits that walk know who you are. Be careful because they just may stop by to say we see you and know who you are. I have learned through the study of the Scripture that they do know who you are once you gain favor with the Lord. For Harry, at some point in his life as young as he was, he has sincerely cried out unto the Lord and was heard. I don't know if this was his first interaction with the spirit realm. I do know I believe him when he says he heard that noise, and like it or not, he had been drafted into the war, and they (evil spirits) do know who you are. I believe he heard what I heard because we were walking the same path although we were not aware of it. From then to now Harry has become a powerful warrior for the Lord, amen.

As for me, that event stays with me. That sound is locked in my mind. Every now and then I remember the fear… the hopelessness of that moment. You would think by now, understanding as I do now, this would have gone away but it has not. You see, now that my faith covers me, the Holy Spirit walks with me all the time. It is an enormous comfort to know these things. It puts you in a place where you no longer fear death because you know your destination in heaven is guaranteed. Once you are saved by Jesus Christ, having accepted his eternal blessing, there is a comfort that comes as your faith grows.

But what we have to understand is that we are here to help others, not ourselves. We are empowered to fight the forces of evil so that we can bring as many souls as possible home to the Lord. And every now and then, we are required to do a self-check. Jesus said that his people will have his father's laws written on their hearts and that it is the heart of a man, not the actions of a man, that the Lord will judge. These laws are called the 10

Commandments, and if, while performing your self-check that you find any of these laws not being followed, then do what's necessary to get them back in line. Failing one commandment will separate you from the Lord.

It is true that once saved always saved. No man can pluck you from the Father's hand once you are saved. We have to understand the rules of salvation because they are not arbitrary and they are nonnegotiable. All 10 Commandments must be present in your heart. If they are not, then you have not been saved. This is not from me, but this is from the Lord. I remind you again that all 10 Commandments must be present in your heart without exception to be saved.

An important note I have discovered throughout my life's walk is that many people don't understand repentance. So, let's make it simple. When you repent, this means that you are telling the Lord that you understand that your actions have been against him and wrong willingly. You are telling him that you are asking for forgiveness for all you have done outside of his will. Make sure that you understand that this is necessary for your salvation. If you can say to yourself that you know you have done wrong, yet if given the chance to do it again, you would do the same thing… Then you have not been forgiven. I have spoken to those who said I meant to do that, and I know it was wrong, but that's what I wanted. People, that is called holding on to sin and letting it be known that if you don't want it to be forgiven? It will not be forgiven. The goal of repentance is to let the Lord know that you are sincere and understand that you have sinned against him, and that is not acceptable. If you hold on to the sins and say I want to be forgiven for everything but that! Then Heaven's Gate will not open for you. There is no room for sin in the kingdom of the Lord, amen.

Entry #6: God's Saving Grace

John 3:16

King James Version

16 For God so loved the world, that he gave his only begotten Son, that whosoever believeth in him should not perish, but have everlasting life.

I like the title of this one because it is about the day I truly got saved. You might think that after all I had been through, I was already saved, and you would be kind of right. I got saved the first time when I was seven years old at Torrance Chapel AME.

My grandmother Long had told us that it was time to get saved, and that was what we were going to do on Sunday. When they had an alter call, she told me and my cousin Vincent to go down there and listen to the minister, so that's what we did. Unfortunately, we did not know why we did it. I remember answering the questions, but I was really following what Vincent was saying. I understood that getting saved meant that your place in heaven was secure, but as to why and how, well, that was missing from the equation for both of us.

We talked about it briefly, but Vincent didn't have any answers, and all I had was questions.

The adults were happy, and we were not about to ruin this by saying we didn't know what had just happened, so we kept our questions to ourselves and moved on.

You might think that given everything I had been through up to this point, getting saved was the next logical, progressive step for me, but it was not. I had so many questions, and so much was happening that getting saved just added to the confusion. The entanglement created by puberty just made trying to understand things harder.

I was convinced that getting saved was something that had to be done repeatedly, so I had a repeated experience again at age 12. As I continued to seek understanding, I got misinformation, bad information, and lies from all directions. Compounding this were arguments, fights, and threats. My daughter Amaris recently said to me as we were discussing the news, "When you have a choice between fear and faith, and you choose fear, that fear now becomes your faith." Those were sound words of wisdom coming from such a young woman, and I told her so. It also defined my teenage years.

I had gotten caught up in the street violence and the confusion the world offered. I watched and read the news intently, preparing for the dangers ahead, both seen and unseen. I had decided that the things that were happening all around me were not going to happen to me. In order to stem such actions, I would need to maintain a defensive posture until action was necessary. I heard the tales of racial hate and witnessed many of them firsthand. At age 12, a Huntersville police officer pulled a gun on me because he thought I stole a case of sandwich ham from Cashion's (A local food market). How did he think that? Was it because all I had on was a tee shirt and shorts, and I was carrying a basketball, which was bizarre? My grandmother's telling of her cousin who was hanged near the JC Smith campus for supposedly dating a white woman. The KKK rides that came through the neighborhood, armed with shotguns and rifles, throwing out pamphlets of what would happen if we tried to "be better than them." The killing of Dr. King. I heard my grandfather say, "If they will kill him, the rest of us are nothing to them." Due to the lack of a better choice, fear had become my faith. I may have had salvation, but salvation didn't have me.

Defend! Prepare! Fight! The anger! The fear! It was what drove

me to believe a final attack was inevitable. I was afraid of the world, and my bad attitude reflected that. I had become so confrontational that some people avoided dealing with me. I wasn't alone. This activity reverberated through the black-oppressed neighborhoods with nicknames like Gun Smoke, The Bottom, The Hill, and so on. Where I lived in Potts Town, we had no paved roads, and most homes didn't have running water until the county decided that the perfect place to put the landfill was Potts Town; after all, black people and trash go together, right? They are used to it.

I remember the adults demanding that the county pave all the roads, not just the one that leads to the dump, and provide running water to all the homes. This was 1970. All the homes never got running water, but they did hand out flyers about rodent control along with a complimentary mouse trap.

All this and more kept the neighborhood on edge. But God was there, or it would have been worse.

August 14, 1976

I was pitching horseshoes when the first rumor came to me. Benit (one of the guys from the neighborhood) had been talking about how bad I thought I was and how he could take me. I did okay, ignoring the rumor mill, but the reports about the same person from three different sources activated my defense protocol.

My thought was, "Why would Benit be jaw-jacking about me? We had no beef. Secondly, if he is, I need to shut him up before one of my older brothers hears about it. There was no need to get smacked by one of them over a big mouth." I found Benit near the dirt basketball court and approached him.

Me, "Hey man, I heard you got something you want to say to me?"

Benit, "Not really, but you do think you are bad. You threw Trace in the bushes last week. Ant man, he my cousin."

Me, "Tell yo cousin that he is lucky I didn't dump him in the trash for throwing a rock at me."

Benit, "He says he didn't throw it at you. He says he was just throwing rocks, and you walked by."

Me, "Yeah, OK. I told him to stop, and he threw another one anyway. After it bounced and hit me, he got his ass whooped. So, now what?"

Benit, "Ant, back up off me!"

Benit wasn't a fighter; he was a talker, and we both knew that. Being a big teen (6'1", 190 pounds), he was easy to take to the ground. At this point in my life, I had been fighting adults in the Charlotte area. A teen was easy pickings. He was trying to keep me from hitting him in the face. He kept trying to cover up, just wanting to survive the attack. I finally trapped his hand and was about to deliver the first of many blows when I heard an unfamiliar voice say, "One day, you are going to meet someone just like you!'

I paused and looked around at the crowd. The voice didn't fit anyone watching the street spectacle. I looked at Benit. He was still trying to cover up, yelling, "Stop! Get off me!" I surveyed the crowd again. I couldn't place the voice, but I did hear it. I got up and reached down to help him up, but he shied away from me with good reason. I wasn't really mad at him, but part of street justice is the intimidation factor. The message being sent is always the same: "This could be you." As I walked through the crowd, I heard murmuring, "Ant chickened out. He had him. Ant's scared of him." I had heard it before. Some of it I had said myself, so I understood the street. It has no leniency. It is unforgiving.

As I walked home, I was confused. Who was that voice? It was the first time a voice spoke to me; that was new. This was not the voice of old. This new voice warned me about me. "You are going to meet someone just like you," it said. That frightened me because that would mean our fears would cause us to fight until death. That has to change. If I am God's warrior, attacking innocent people is wrong. Attacking anyone is wrong unless it is a defensive action, but how do I change this? I asked God to help me. I got home, but no one was there. God did not answer me. That is usually the way when you already know the answer. I saw the Bible on the coffee table where it always was and started to read, "In the beginning there was God...

I don't remember how long it took me to read, but I stopped when Rev Billy Graham Crusade came on. My mom used to always watch him. I would listen for a while but eventually tune it out. I remembered black preachers talking about him and saying they didn't trust him because he was white. For me, color was not something I could use to judge a man's worth. If you look closely, you will see that no two have the exact same color scheme. God uses color as an identifier. This is who you are and what you look like. It does not make you smarter, faster, or give you superpowers. Just an identifier and it is only for you. It won't rub off and cannot be transferred.

As Rev. Graham started to preach, I was amazed. For the first time, I understood every word! He was crystal clear, and it captivated me. I followed him as he spoke and taught. As often as I had been in church, and believe me, it was a lot, never had I understood a man better. When he got to the end, he called those who wanted to be saved to pray with him, and I understood because he made it so clear. Once saved, always saved. No one can pick you out of God's hand, he said. Accept Jesus as your Lord and Savior. Jesus is undefeated, for He has conquered death and is the key to eternal life. No man may go to the Father except by me! Will you come?

Rev. Graham had me at "Undefeated." That's the team I want to be on—like the 72 Dolphins! Flippers team! Undefeated. Sign me up! I hardly slept that night. I read and read the scriptures that night and thanked Rev. Graham for being the most anointed of the Most High God. He saved thousands, and I am proud to be one of them.

It felt awesome to finally have a deeper understanding of what being saved meant. Understanding that it only has to happen once and last forever made sense to me. Also, knowing that repentance and forgiveness were part of the process gave me a clearer understanding.

I woke the next morning wondering what church was going to be like, and it was the same as usual. Nothing changed except my awareness of being saved. I expected that someone would see the difference in me, but no one did. Later that day, I watched the news, and I noticed that the fear of what was happening on the TV was gone. I didn't feel like I had to arm and protect myself anymore. I was surprised at the feeling. God really was my protector, and I could relax in that truth. It felt good. I felt good. Sunday was good for me. I watched Rev. Graham's crusade again. More understanding was what I wanted, and he delivered. Little did I know that Monday was coming and all of this would change again.

On Monday after school, I was at the neighborhood gym, playing basketball. We played at Torrence-Lytle, the old black school for grades 1-12. I never got to attend because that was the first year of integration, and I attended Davidson Elementary.

While we were playing, one of the guys, Neil, threw an elbow. I caught his elbow and shoved him out of bounds. Without looking, he turned and swung, hitting me on the right side of my neck. Everybody stopped. Neil saw that it was me he hit. He covered up and dropped to the floor. My first thought was to kick him, but it was quickly replaced with a new thought, which was to let him go. Forgive him. This was an accident. I wasn't sure what to do. Attacking had become second nature, but this time, I didn't want to attack. Jesus said, "Love your enemy and turn the other cheek." I already knew that, but putting it into practice was new to me. The people I had witnessed turning the other cheek were turning it because somebody was beating on the other one.

Everyone was waiting for the next move. I said, "I'm going to let that go." Neil didn't believe me so he didn't move. I reached out my hand to help him up, and he flinched because he thought I was going to hit him. I said, "Come on! Get up!" He got up on his own and stepped away from me. I said, "Play ball. Ball up! Take it out!" Neil said to me, "Ant, I didn't mean to…" I cut him off, "I know. Don't let it happen again!" Then I laughed, and everybody else laughed. It changed the mood. Inside, I was burning with the need to body-slam him. I was at war with myself. If he swings again, do I attack? Guys are going to think I have gone soft, but if they do, I will attack. But how can you attack and forgive at the same time? This forgiveness and the cheek-turning thing was confusing. I needed more information. I needed prayer.

I was trying to figure this thing out. I prayed and got nothing. I searched the scriptures and found plenty of God's warriors, but there was no instruction or guidance that helped me. Reading about Samson was fun, but meeting with some chick and getting my fro cut off was neither available nor a wonton option. So, I turned to my trusty old World Book Encyclopedias.

A trusted source if there ever was one. First, I looked up warrior. I knew the ones from TV and the movies were too scripted. Searching warriors only told me that warriors protected the land and fought off invaders unless they were the invaders. My research continued until I found knights who served the king, but suddenly, I found a clue. A group of special knights who dedicated themselves to serving God. No name was given, so I turned to the dictionary and found Holy fighters by several names, but the best was called Paladins. Back to the World Books, where I found Paladins started in France but became a force to be reckoned with, and their purpose was to return the lands and items that belonged to God back to Him in the battles called crusades. A noble cause, I guess, but not something I was going to do.

After spending several days researching all this, I determined that the Paladin's duty to serve God was good enough for me to adopt as my own. To me, it meant curving aggression, defending the weak and oppressed, following the Ten Commandments, and living by the Golden Rule. I needed my own personal mantra, and I found it. It was: Be not the bully but be the bully hunter. I liked it.

In the days and weeks to come, I had taken on this new understanding of what a Paladin was. I broke up fights instead of encouraging or ignoring them. I stopped reacting to rumors and loudmouths, well, to rumors anyway. Loud mouths had to be quieted. They would be the exception. Turning the other cheek was always a tricky thing, but I did it. It was necessary because Jesus ordered it. There was just one thing left to correct to clear my honor. Neil would have to be dealt with again.

Neil, for some reason, thought I was afraid of him and had been saying just that. I really could care less about it, but the streets won't let it die so easily. After all, he did get a free swing on me. For the purpose of stats, Neil was all of 5'5", about 130 pounds wet. Me? 6'2" 200 pounds. With the fear gone, God had internally naturalized my aggressiveness. I like the calmer me. No more looking over my shoulder. Jesus said He would never leave nor forsake me, and I took that to heart, but my brothers, Grayling in particular, did not. He wanted something done about Neil, so I came up with a solution. I would confront Neil and set the record straight.

That Saturday, there was a softball game, and Neil was there, so I went over to him.

Me, "Sup man."

Neil, "Nothin. Sup!"

Me, "Neil, do you think I am scared of you or something?"

Neil, "No. We cool, Ant man."

Me, "Well, I keep hearing that. Maybe you think because you hit me, I don't hit back no more. Is that it? That what you think?"

Neil, "Wellll, nah! Ant man. I was just playing (snickering)."

That snicker told me all I needed to know. Sometimes, the law of the jungle is the last law to use, but it is real, and it is necessary sometimes. So, I stepped up to Neil and said, "I believe you have been running off with the mouth. I believe that you are stupid and can't help yourself. Now, this is what is about to happen. The next words that I don't like and you say, are going to get you dogged right here, right now! Do you have anything to say?" Neil shook his head no. I continued, "Ok. Now, I gave you a pass that day because I felt sorry for you. I turned the other cheek because there is no honor in winning a fight that you are supposed to win. It's sorta like fighting a girl if I fight you, but your mouth is writing a check…You get me, Neil man!"

Neil nodded yes.

I walked away. We never had another disagreement, and we are still friends. I also apologized to Benit years later. When I told him about what he said when we were fighting, he said, "You heard me say what? I didn't say nothing to you. I couldn't. I was trying to keep you from hitting me. You were crazy back then, Ant. Couldn't nobody say nothing to you. You were just fighting all the time. I don't know what you heard, but I'm glad you heard it."

Me, "So, what did I hear?"

Benit, "I'own know. Knowing you, it was God. It wasn't the devil cause he would have cheered you on. Look at the change though Ant. You went from big and bad to just big." We laughed. We agreed the voice was right. Fear was no longer my faith.

I now know that voice was the voice of my guardian angel, warning me of impending doom if I continued down the wrong path. We have shared many visions together now, and he even gave me his name. That is a story for the third book. He shook my tree because it was falling. I pray for all who have allowed fear to become their faith. Find Jesus and get saved before your guardian angel has to shake your tree.

Entry #7: I am number 22, but that's not what the Lord said

November 1977

I played high school basketball at North Mecklenburg High School near Huntersville, NC, and I also participated in several other sports. This is not a sports story, so I will not indulge you or myself in my sports accolades. Just know that I was an outstanding athlete and received many athletic rewards. I was chosen Athlete of the Decade for the years 1970 – 1980. I just had to get that in (I love it, but it doesn't pay, no money, lol).

This was the first time I met an angel and had a vision, and in that vision, the angel answered the prayer for me. I know there are going to be many who would say why the Lord answered such a small prayer that meant little to nothing to anyone except the person praying. This encounter helped to let me know that for every little prayer that is made, God hears. He responds in one of three ways: yes, no, or not right now. The good thing is he always responds, but for us mortals, only the yes is what we want to hear. Many times, I will get a yes, but it is also followed by not right now. The good thing about this is that the Lord knows when we need what we ask for. We get our general daily blessings that all men receive every day.

For those who believe and worship the Lord there are additional blessings and protections that we get each day. For the Lord says he blesses the just and the unjust, the righteous and the unrighteous:

Matthew 5:44-46

King James Version

44 But I say unto you, love your enemies, bless them that curse you, do good to them that hate you, and pray for them which despitefully use you, and persecute you;

45 That ye may be the children of your Father which is in heaven: for he maketh his sun to rise on the evil and on the good, and sendeth rain on the just and on the unjust.

46 For if ye love them which love you, what reward have ye? do not even the publicans the same?

It is in this verse that the Lord lets us know that is easy to love those that you are already familiar with. To love someone who was a stranger or an enemy or just simply an adversary is hard for us to do, for we are mortal, and being moral, we will forever be protective of our mortality. We are now in the end times and it has become so dangerous that when we walk among each other, we now need to keep our heads on a swivel. Those who have nothing to do with one another reach out and cause incalculable damage. This cannot be ignored, and in case you haven't already guessed it, I am one of those who is for gun control. Advocating for the removal of assault-killing weapons from the general public and relegating this only to law enforcement is our best option.

I do agree with the right to bear arms, just not arms that would kill King Kong. Since King Kong doesn't exist, we don't need King Kong-style weapons to coexist with one another. There are more than enough handguns and long guns available for anyone to use who can pass the registrations and restrictions and still protect themselves. I know I've heard the tales. I need a gun to protect myself from a burglar or carjacking and the like. I could be wrong, but I have never heard of a burglar using an AR-15 to burglarize someone's home. Such a large gun would just get in the way. As children of God, we mislead by setting the example by first putting forth the golden rule of do unto others as you would have them do unto you and then following that up with love your neighbors as I have loved you.

I had made the varsity basketball team at North Meck as a freshman. This was an unexpected success for me. I had quit the junior high school team because of prejudice issues. The coach of the junior high school team had promised me that I would not make the high school team. I attempted to play in the Optimist League again. In the one game that I played in, I scored 53 points and three-quarters of play. The coach told me there was no competition in this league for me, and it would be unfair to the league for me to continue to compete against those who were not going to increase my skill. So, I was left with no place to play except on my own.

One of the guys from the neighborhood, whose nickname was Cheese, gave me some good advice. Cheese advised me to work on my game. He said one thing you need to work on is your left-hand because anytime someone tries to defend you from the left side, you either spend to your right and shoot or you take a fast step in and shoot. He said you pretty much have perfected that move, and you go so high when you make that spin. That bounce, that it still makes you difficult to defend, but when they pick you up full court on your left side, you hesitate because you're not in shooting range, so you're going to have to work on that. When you broke your right hand, it was probably the best thing for you as far as increasing your left-hand abilities. So, I went to the library and got a book on basketball. It had shooting forms, dribbling techniques, rebounding techniques, and passing techniques. I use this book religiously every day in preparation for next year's school basketball tryouts. And the payoff was incredible! But again, this is not an athletic story, so I will progress.

It was good that I made the varsity team. However, I became very ill during the tryouts. I barely remember the final day. I had contracted both the flu and the measles, and this was not good. I remember my cousin Rodney coming over to me because I was lying on the bench sweating profusely. He said, "Ant, you made the team!" I said, "That's great." Then Rodney said, "I mean, you made the varsity team!" I said, "The varsity? Why?" Rodney said, "Because you were putting on a show. The coach said you can make your shot on anybody!" This was happy news for me and unhappy news for me. It was happy news because making the varsity as a freshman is rare at any high school. But all my friends were on the JV team. That's who I wanted to play with, but it just goes to show one's lack of understanding of high school athletics. Gone were the days of playing just to have fun. Now. this thing was about making money and making a run for a state championship. Folk's, high school sports in North Carolina are serious business.

Although I made it to the varsity team, I would not play on the team this year. My illness was so severe that I was quarantined at home for the measles and missed 33 days of school. By the time I got back to school, the season had started. Missing so many days meant that I should have been held back for that year. But after much testing and testing and testing again it was determined that although I was

123

missing those days, I should be allowed to continue with my original graduating class of 1980. It's what I wanted and to this day we still have the best Annual Cover of any class that has ever graduated as a Viking! Yeah, it's like that!

Now that I was back with the JV team, which is where I wanted to be, I needed a jersey and a number. For me I had already made up my mind that my numbers should be 22. Why 22? That was the number of my favorite football player, Mercury Morris, with the Miami Dolphins. This was going to be my highlight! I was going to be Mercury Morris on the basketball team. Juke them, jab them, shake 'em down, and shoot it in their face, and if you press me, I'm going to dunk in your mug! This is who I was on the court and I liked it. Coach Holden was the varsity coach but in truth, he managed both teams.

Upon my return, Coach explained that the season it started and that bringing me up now would be tough because I missed all of preseason. I understood. I didn't want to be on the varsity anyway, but things work out for the best in many cases. Coach told me to report to the gym the next day and pick out my jersey number. I immediately replied, "I'll take 22!" He said we will see what's left because there is not much.

That evening while at my grandparents' house, my grandfather asked me about making the team even after being sick. My grandfather was the custodian at North Meck High. So, the teachers and the coaches had been talking to him about my performance on the court. It made him proud and I like to see the smile on his face. My grandfather meant a lot to me and he always encouraged me to do better and try harder. He really didn't understand how basketball really worked because when he was growing up, blacks weren't allowed to play basketball. He said he would see white people playing, but they weren't allowed to be on the court.

Pop, "They tell me that you dump the ball real good!" (While laughing at the dinner table)

Me, "Yes Sir, but It's called dunking the ball." (I was Laughing too)

Pop, "Oh! Is that what they were saying? Whatever it is, you do it real good."

Me: "Yes sir, that's what they tell me. I get to pick my jersey number tomorrow."

Pop, "And what number are you going to pick?"

Me, "I'm going to pick 22."

Pop, "Why number 22?"

Me, "Because my favorite football player wears 22 so I'm going to wear 22!"

Pop, "Is that the only reason?"

Me, "Yes, is there another reason?"

Pop, "Out of all the years that you have gone to church, you haven't figured out that numbers mean something. God uses numbers to get things done. You know seven days a week? That has meaning. This guy who was number 22? Your favorite player? I'll bet that number means something to him. Do you know what it means to him?"

Me, "Nope, I just know he's awesome! When I put that number 22 on, I'm gonna be awesome too!"

Pop, "Did you ask the Lord about this? The Lord's done some mighty things for you for you to make this decision without talking about it to him."

I found this a little odd for my grandfather. He normally didn't go down this road, but his being a minister and being aware of how God uses numbers woke something up in him that day, so I started to pay more attention.

Me, "So you think God has a number for me? And that number is not 22?"

Pop, "Well, you have to ask him about that but I would believe he has a number for you. Why don't you pray about it and see what he says."

So, I took my grandfather's advice and decided I would pray tonight and see what happened. That night, when I went to bed, I prayed and asked God to give me the number that he wanted me to have. I did happen to mention that He would want me to have the number 22. That night, I had my first vision as a teenager. In that vision, I was given my number and told what it would do for me.

The Vision

I found myself standing in the sanctuary at Torrance Chapel AME. This was the church that my mom went to and I consider it my home church. My grandfather preached at the House of Prayer. I looked around because I was trying to figure out was this real? And might actually be in church? It looked real but there was no one there. I looked at my hands just to see if there was real, and apparently, they were. This was new for me. I had heard about visions but I'm not sure I understood what one really was. I definitely didn't think I was going to have one.

Acts 2:16-18

King James Version

16 But this is that which was spoken by the prophet Joel;

17 And it shall come to pass in the last days, saith God, I will pour out of my Spirit upon all flesh: and your sons and your daughters shall prophesy, and your young men shall see visions, and your old men shall dream dreams:

18 And on my servants and on my handmaidens, I will pour out in those days of my Spirit; and they shall prophesy:

I used to hear in church about people having visions and interacting with other people in those visions. The only people I actually believed had visions were those of the Bible. I had no idea how wrong I was going to be. I have had so many visions, and I know many others who have had visions, that it's incredible. It simply means God is at work constantly on our behalf, all the time, every time.

As I stood there in front of the pulpit, I became aware of a presence standing on my left side. I could see him slightly from the corner of my eye. He was huge and he was given off this radiant feeling of comfort. He wasn't glowing and I could not see his face. That radiant energy he gave off was so powerful and soothing. I kept trying to see him, to look at him, but it was not possible. He finally moved. I still could not see him but I could see his hands. He had a golden box that glowed a bright golden light. This golden light surrounded the box but it was not emanating from the box. It had these sparkly things all around it, not like on TV. I looked at the box and then he spoke:

Angel, "This is for you!" (In a very deep baritone voice)

Me, "What is it?"

Angel, "It is what you asked for. It is for you."

Slowly, the box opened, and a number in bright golden light was in the box, and that number was (drumroll please) number 33. It was beautiful. The numbers were etched on what appeared to be a block of gold bullion. The container floated in the air, but it was still in the box. The angel said, "Take it." As I reached in and picked the number up, it had no weight, but it moved, tilting a little back and forth. As I held it the angel continued to speak:

Angel, "While you wear this number, you will be protected and you will perform to the best of your ability. This is the number that the Lord has chosen for you."

The vision ended with a fade-to-black moment. I sat up in my bed, still trying to figure out if this was a vision or a dream. It was different than any dream I had ever had. It didn't feel like a dream, and that angel's presence seemed to be the major difference to me. I replayed this over and over in my head all day. I told some of the guys about it, of course, everybody was wild about it, but nobody seemed to be stunned.

After I arrived at practice, Coach Holden asked me what jersey number that I wanted. He was standing in the equipment room:

Coach, "Well have you made up your mind?"

Me, "Yes! I want number 22!"

Coach, "We said that's what you wanted and a good thing is we got it!"

Me, "Sweet!"

Coach rumbled around in the room a little bit and found jersey number 22.

Coach, "I don't think you gon'na like this. But here you go."

He held up jersey number 22 and it looked like something you would put on a small child; Coach was laughing. Seeing that I was 6'2 weighing 200 pounds this was not going to work. Now, I was thinking should I ask for 33? I know that's what was in the vision, but as a 16-year-old, I really didn't understand the power and the direction that visions are meant to take you. The coach, laughing and looking around, said, "Let's see what I have back here that will fit you." Coach continued to rummage through a box and then he pulled out this jersey and said, "This is the only one that is going to fit you." It was number 33. While I was still surprised that I was getting number 33, it wasn't unexpected. The funny thing is, Rodney (my cousin), whom I had told about the vision, walked over to me, looked at the jersey, and said, "You're stupid. Did you really think He gave you that vision for nothing? After all the stuff that God has put you through! He gives you a number, and you pick something different, and you thought He was gonna let that go? You see he didn't pick anybody else's number, just yours." Then he plucked me on the ear and I said, "Do that again, you going to be eating dirt!" As Rodney walked away, he just yelled out, "Stupid!"

I put my jersey on and walked over to the mirror. This looked good on me. I liked it. I got those double digits ya'll. When I told my grandfather what happened, he said, "That's what I was trying to tell you. Ask the Lord about your ways, and He will direct you. Ask the Lord about your wants, and he will guide you. Y'all act like you don't know what to do but you go to church all the time."

I didn't want to go into it any further because it would've struck a nerve. What my grandfather did not understand is that when we were in church, we weren't being taught, we were being yelled at. Between the hooping and the chanting, the young people were lost. For me personally, it wasn't until I listened to Billy Graham on television that I understood for the first time what a preacher was supposed to sound like. I understood him clearly, cleanly, and deeply. Although I love my grandfather with all my heart, Billy Graham became my favorite preacher. I would never miss a chance to hear Billy Graham preach.

Entry #8: The Visitors, a.k.a. Am I being Watched?

Luke 21:25-26

King James Version

[25] And there shall be signs in the sun, and in the moon, and in the stars; and upon the earth distress of nations, with perplexity; the sea and the waves roaring;

[26] Men's hearts failing them for fear, and for looking after those things which are coming on the earth: for the powers of heaven shall be shaken.

Now, I believe I have been fully drafted by the Lord to fight on his behalf in his army. As a child, this felt really good to me. I believed in some fashion that I now had a unique protection and direction that was unstoppable. Not in the sense that I was invincible, but I felt that because God had called me his warrior, then I was going to have to fight evil, for he is good and does not represent evil at any point in time. Now I just needed to wait for my direction to be determined.

I present to you my first UFO encounter. In my wildest dreams, I would've never thought that something like this would happen to me. The good thing is it didn't just happen to me, it happened to several people in the neighborhood and out of the neighborhood, from what I am told. I have developed a theory as to what people call these types of encounters. My theory is not among the common ones. Because there were several factors that I had to consider in order to accept what happened.

I will get into my theories after the story because then it will make more sense. I was happy when my sister saw it because it made her stop saying, "Ant is seeing little green men." Trust me, that statement made me mad because I didn't see any men of any kind just the object. For good measure, as of the year 2023, she is the only person I know who saw a UFO. She actually saw two on her way home from work. They flew by her while she sat at a red light. More information on that later but I do believe her that there be no doubt of that.

December 25, 1976 – 6:15 PM

Christmas Day, I love it so much. We used to decorate the lights off the roof, literally. We had lights on the fence, in the yard, on the trees, on the porch, on the house, along with Santa Claus, reindeer, and candy canes; and inside the house, there was a silver Christmas tree with a colored wheel in front of it. This was my grandmother's house and she spared no expense. It was beautiful and so were the other houses in the neighborhood. People used to come by and take pictures, and my mom's house was no different. Decorate it to the hilt and Christmas Day would be the last day those lights will shine until the new year starts.

Putting them up was a pain but the results were stunning. If that happened with today's equipment you would've been able to see the house from the moon. At this time of the day, I was at my grandparents still eating Christmas dinner. I had just inhaled another turkey leg when the dog lost his mind and started barking at the tree in front of the house like he was crazy. In the living room were my grandparents, Uncle James, Aunt Gracie, and my cousins Josie and Gwynne.

Gwynee and I were in the kitchen. She was complaining to me about trying to eat everything. I was ignoring her as I always did and continuing to eat. My Uncle James and his family lived in New York and would come down during the holidays. Because we only saw them during the holidays, it was a special time for my grandparents. They would lay out all the bells and whistles, and whatever anybody else wanted didn't count. And we were forced to play with our younger cousins whether we liked it or not. So, the food was part of the bribe to get us to get up there and play with them. But the feeling was mutual- they did not want to play with us either. They were more than happy to hang out with my sister, and I was more than happy to have them hang out with my sister. But my sister was 18 years old, and she didn't want to hang out with them. She would do it for a little while, but then she would break out and do what 18-year-olds do which is not to play with 10-year-olds.

So, what was left was for the next youngest person, being me, and one of my brothers to be guardians and playmates for our younger cousins. Because my brothers did not have the patience for this, I normally became the fall guy. Somehow this worked because I did have fun. I had learned over the years that if I wanted to get something, I would have one of them ask for it. This worked like a charm! More food for the brother. I just had to be able to put up with the endless questioning as to why I was doing anything.

The dog, Shep was his name, was a German Shepherd who guarded the yard well. But right then I was standing in the kitchen looking at him barking at the tree. Since it was not a car, he did not have to chase it, and considering all things, it had already been caught. Why was he barking at the tree? Personally, I didn't care. It wasn't as if he was disturbing me; I was focused on food. Then I heard from the living room, my grandfather (from this point known as Pop) yell at me to go shut the dog up! My first thought was, "Me? He's not my dog. He's G-man's (my older brother Gray) dog!" And since he's not here then the dog authority should fall to my grandfather because that's who the dog actually belonged. So, I did what most 14-year-olds do which is nothing. I hope the dog was shut up but he didn't. Shep continued his frantic barking at the tree. I continued to eat, and Gwynee continued to ask questions about my food intake.

As Shep continued to bark even I started to take notice. 'What the heck is his problem? He's gonna cause me some work.' I know what. What I needed to do was to finish and leave or else I was going to be put to work. Unfortunately for me, my appetite would not let me leave so I go toward the potato pie. My intention was to eat half of this very quickly before Gwynee could rat me out. But I didn't make it. Pop yelled for me to shut the dog up with a lot more force this time, so I could not ignore him.

I walked to the front door, and I noticed Gwynee did not follow. I looked back in the kitchen, and she was glaring at the sweet potato pie. I knew she didn't want it, but just in case, I did need to redirect a new claim for the pie.

Me, "Don't touch it."

Gwynee, "I don't want your, stupid pie! You eat too much anyway!"

Me, "Yeah right! Just don't touch it! I know you!"

Pop, "I told you to shut the dog up!"

Me, "It's not my dog, but I know. Shut the dog up!"

I put on my coat and went onto the porch and I just stared at the dog for a minute. I was thinking what is his deal? I said twice, "Shut up! Shep actually looked back and then continued to bark at the tree. I hear the door close and Gwynee is now standing behind me on the porch. It was not unusual for her to follow me but it was irritating. Gwynee was four years younger than me. So, she being 10 and me being 14 was not a match for cousins to hang out together. Just as an update, we created a bond that later into adulthood became something I kin to brother and sister. I say this to all the cousins who are in my predicament. Hang in there, God has a plan for this relationship to blossom into something so good; you cannot imagine it. Love you Gwynee! The next time you hit me pow! Zoom!

Me, "What do you want?"

Gwynee, "I want to see what you are doing."

Me, "You're just being nosy."

Gwynee, "You are being sneaky. I know you trying to sneak off, so wherever you go, I'm going too!"

Me, "I'm not trying to sneak off. If I want to leave, I leave, and you can't go so you can take that coat off and go back in the house."

Gwynee, "You don't tell me what to do and if you try to leave I'm telling!"

Me, "Yeah you do that best. Tell! I can see it now! Capt. Tell it! No one is safe!"

She punched me in the side. If I had punched her back, she would have landed in Europe. I walked over to the dog who was still barking like crazy at this tree. I grabbed him by the collar and pulled him back and told him to stop barking and to be quiet. He was not really listening and I noticed he was looking at something up in the tree. I looked up in the tree and I saw nothing. So, I pet him, hoping to calm him down. Then Gwynee spoke.

Gwynee, "Ant what color is the moon?"

Me, "Why are you asking me such a stupid question."

Gwynee, "I'm not stupid, and you're supposed to know all the stuff about science, but you don't know what color the moon is."

That statement ticked me off! How dare a 10-year-old question my knowledge of the cosmos! She really was begging for a trip to Europe via left hook. Now I'm aggravated by the dog. I'm aggravated by the cousin. I can't eat my pie and the fact that she is pretending like she doesn't know what color the moon is makes it worse! She's doing this just to aggravate me more and it's working so I turned to her and looked down at her and I said in a rough voice:

Me, "You know what color the moon is! Don't! Ask me! That again!"

You would think that when your 6'2 ", 200 lb older, very athletic cousin issues what has to be seen as a clear threat, you would back off! But she didn't even flinch; she just continued, which was even more irritating because she was convinced I would not knock her into Europe! This is always the case; threatening her was like talking to a wall; she just didn't believe it. She had no fear. And that is still the case today.

Gwynee, "Is that the moon?" (She was pointing into the sky which would be northeast)

Me, "Yes that's the moon. Why are you asking me this?"

Gwynee, "Then what is that?" She was now pointing directly over our heads and what I saw froze me in amazement! There was an object directly over the house. It was huge. It was not making a sound. I could no longer even hear the dog barking. My mind tried to calculate what this thing was but there was no calculation to be done. I have no idea what the heck that thing was. At first, I thought it could be a weather balloon, but I knew what a weather balloon looked like, and I knew a weather balloon would not be floating over my grandparents' house. Then I hear:

Gwynee, "Ant is that the moon, too?"

Me, "No, that ain't the moon!"

Gwynee, "Then what is it? Do you know what that is?"

Me, "I know it's not the moon. The earth doesn't have two moons, especially one right there."

I turned to see the moon and I saw it was still where it was before. I looked back at the object that was just sitting. I looked back at the moon then looked back at the object and I realized this was a UFO or potentially one. Since I had no data on what a UFO would look like in person, I did not know how to classify what I was seeing. It was big and elongated, similar to that of a cigar but it did not have a round end. I needed to see more of it because of its size. I could not view the whole thing from my vantage point, so I decided to go outside the fence to get a better view. Gwynee was becoming frantic now that

I decided to move. She grabbed me by my arm and started pulling me back away from the fence. I grabbed her arm, and I told her to turn me loose. As I started to walk toward the gate, Gwynee started screaming:

Gwynee, "No! Ant stop! You can't go out there! That thing is going to get you! You can't go out there! You don't know what that is and it's gonna get you! Ant please stop! Don't go out there is after you! Please don't go!"

Me, "Did you get a camera for Christmas? Give it here! Give me your camera!"

Gwynee, "No! Stop don't go! You do not get my camera and you're not going! That thing is going to get you! It's after you!"

Her frantic pleas for the first time let me know of a concern for my safety. I looked at her and I said, "It's not after me. It is just sitting there." I grabbed the camera from a pocket and told her to go inside. I went out of the fence and into the road. Gwynee ran into the house yelling that I was following something into the street (her New York accent is now in full effect). As I went into the street, I started to get a good view of how big this thing was; it was huge but it was not making a sound. I took pictures, this was going to be good. As I moved out into the street further, the object started to move. I was taking pictures and the object repositioned itself directly over my head. I now had a full view of this thing. It was actually flat on the bottom, although from my original point of view, it looked cigar-shaped. It was actually more about oval with a flat bottom. Our tree at that time was approximately 35 feet high, the object was nearly on top of the tree.

As it moved over me I could see colors swirling around the object. I thought maybe someone was playing a joke, and I probably should've already been running. I wondered if this was a projection of some type.

I looked for a light source, but there was none. Now that I could see the entire thing, I looked for any signs of anything accompanying this object, but there was none. I then looked to see if this object had windows. It had squares that could be a possible window. There were six of them but they weren't open as a window would be or nothing that I would have defined as a window. It was metallic and the colors swirled from a light orange and yellow to a dark orange-yellow, flowing left to right. It was a beautiful work of art but it was still floating over me.

As I moved further out into the street, it moved with

me. When I got to where Ms. Lena lived, I stopped because I was trying to get better pictures, but it kept moving over the top of me, and then it would stop when I stopped. I began to wonder why this object was moving with me. If it was still, I could get better pictures, but it was moving as I moved. I continued to try to outpace the object but I could not. It continued to move. Every time I stopped, it stopped. It was messing up my photo opportunity to get the full view. As I neared the recreational center in the neighborhood, I saw four adults standing in front of Miss Barringer's house at the mailboxes.

It was a place where we gathered and talked. It was in front of the old black high school named Torrance-Lytle. It had been abandoned since the integration of the schools took place in 1968, the very year I would've attended my first grade, they shut it down. My three older siblings had attended and they loved it. I couldn't wait to attend. But it

155

was not meant for me. I attended Davidson Elementary School for my first year, and that was the end of that, back to the story.

As I approached the mailboxes, the four men, Wayne, Hopper, Gene, and Bryce, saw me walking in the middle of the road. As they saw me approach, they started laughing. I saw Wayne nudge Bryce and all four men looked up and started laughing. Then Hopper said:

Hopper, "Ant! Boy, you better get out of the middle of the road before you get run over."

Wayne, "Don't tell him nothing. Stay there till a car comes. He'll move then!"

Gene, "Ant! What are you doing?"

Me, "I'm taking pictures of that!" I pointed above my head. The four men froze and gasped in surprise because they now saw the object above me. Each of the four men ran in a different direction. Bryce ran home because his house was about 50 yards from the mailboxes. This was the only time I thought I was in danger. When full-grown men see something and run, this is a sign in our neighborhood that you should've already been running from whatever it is that they see.

I stopped because now I was thinking this may not be a good idea. But when I stopped, the object stopped, so I looked up, and it was still there. It looked lower than it did before and bigger, but it was still there and was not doing anything to me, so I continued to take pictures. I was still trying to outpace the object, but it continued to move as I moved so it was not happening. I was now at the mailboxes where the four men were. I heard someone call my name from my right and it was three of my cousins, Quentin, Galen, and Amy.

They were near the corner by the Patterson's house. Quentin says to Galen and Amy, "I told you was over Ant's house." Then I heard a voice ring out. It was my Aunt Dot. She was Bryce's mother. She yelled:

Aunt, "Anthony Houston, stop right there!"

I came to an immediate halt, and so did the object.

Aunt, "You leave that thing alone!"

Me, "I'm not doing anything to it! It's just following me down the street."

Aunt Dot, "I said, leave that thing alone! Stay right there where you are!"

So I stopped and of course, the object stopped. More people were seeing it now. I stood still for approximately 30 seconds. Quentin, Amy, and

Galen didn't come any closer. After about 30 seconds, the object began to move, slowly at first. Now, I could get a picture of the back of it. As this thing moved off, I was calculating in my mind if it was going to move the way they said on television or if we were going to actually be able to see where this thing would go. I personally never believed that the zip-away was real. For a craft to move at the reported speeds in our atmosphere was not possible. I knew enough about that from physics to know that as an object moves through the Earth's atmosphere, air compresses in front of it. This compressed air will create friction to the point of catching on fire at some point, not to mention that the breaking of the sound barrier would come first. None of this happened, which made me think that what people were actually seeing was something else. This was why the Silver Surfer could not move at full speed through Earth's atmosphere. I had to throw that in there because I loved my comic books and The Silver Surfer is one of my favorites.

What I witnessed next confounded and confused me for the next several years, but I have a theory we will discuss in a bit. The object continued to move away at a gradual pace. I would say it moved up slightly slowly, deliberately to about 100 feet. At that position, it stopped and started moving again a little faster and then it zipped away! Gone! Right in front of our eyes! It! Simply! Zipped away! Just as all those reports said, it did! At that point, I was stunned and angry.

Whoever or whatever this thing was wanted me to believe that it could just zip through our atmosphere without making a ripple? That is a con job, and I was not accepting it. It thinks we are stupid, but we are not. We may be gullible, but not stupid.

I looked around for residue of some type because this movement was not possible in the Earth's atmosphere without consequences. I knew the people standing around me said, "Did you see that?" And I said, "Yes! I saw that, but that's not possible!" Quentin said:

Quentin, "Did you see that!"

Me, "Yes, I saw it, but Quentin, that is not possible."

Quentin, "Ant, you just saw that thing take off. What do you mean is not possible?"

Me, "What I mean is it can't move throughout the atmosphere like that, Quentin. According to the laws of physics, that's not possible. I witnessed it, but something else has to be present here. There is an unidentified variable at play. We just have to figure out what it is. A solid object cannot move through our atmosphere at zippo speeds. It will cause a fireball of enormous size and a shockwave that will destroy a lot of stuff around here."

Quentin, "So what did we see then? I'm not saying I'm as smart as you, but I do know what I saw, and I know what you saw. That thing zipped out of here with no problem, so maybe your physics laws are wrong."

Me, "No, the physics laws are sound and proven. What's not proven is how a solid object can move through Earth's atmosphere without making a single disturbance. I couldn't find a power source on that object, which means to me that it's using a source that physics cannot account for as we know it."

Amy said, "You are going to find out what that is ain't you?"

Galen, "You know he is. That thing was over your house a long time."

Quentin, "Yeah it was all over your house for a long time. We figured it was looking for you."

Me, "And how did you figure it was looking for me? Where did that idea come from?"

Quentin, "Strange stuff happens to you all the time, don't it? (Turning to Amy and Galen) this don't surprise nobody. You know you're all into that science stuff."

Me, "I know what you're saying, but I don't think that's it. After all, if you got one of those, you don't need any scientific information from me. There's nothing I can do for you to make something like that."

Amy, "Then what do you think it is Ant? It was all over your house for about 30 minutes. Everybody saw that."

Me, "30 minutes? That's how long you saw this thing?"

Quentin, "Yeah, about that before it started moving."

Galen, "It was there for about 10 minutes, and then it started moving down the street. It was not sitting there over the house for 30 minutes, but it came from out of nowhere. It wasn't there, then it was there."

Me, "So you didn't see it come in or arrive like a plane or helicopter? You just looked up because you are always outside playing, and you just saw it there, right?"

All three said yes. That was pertinent information for me because it told me that the way it arrived, it was not a plane or an object that used traditional methods of moving through the atmosphere. This kept me up all night long. I went to the World Book encyclopedias and mentally got lost in studying physics, motion, and motion dynamics. I really could not believe this thing just zipped away. But I have a theory. I will get into that in a minute.

I went back to my grandparents' house and Gwynee was still upset. She came over to me, punched me in my stomach, and said:

Gwynee, "You left me! That thing could've done anything to you! You know those things take people!" She tried to punch me again. I just grabbed a little fist and said stop!

Me, "You see, it didn't take me, so stop! Plus, I got pictures! Lots of pictures! This is going to be good."

Gwynee, "You don't have the pictures. I was trying to tell you that the camera doesn't have any film, so you don't have any pictures."

Me, "What! Why would you have a camera with no film? I can't believe this?"

Aunt Gracie, "She doesn't have any film because all she would do is waste it."

My disappointment was obvious. No film, no pictures, no real proof. Others saw it, but that was all I had. In retrospect, there was a lot of evidence from so many witnesses, but the pictures would've tipped the scale. As it was the next day, I went down to the gym (community center). At some point, my Aunt Dot found out I was there and sent for me. This was during lunch. She lived directly across from the gym so I went over. She may have really good food. I was so hoping that since it was lunchtime, she would make food, and she did well! She said, "Sit down, son. I need to talk to you." So, I sit with a ham sandwich with Kool-Aid. "I am all ears."

Aunt Dot, "Now listen, Bryce told me you were following that thing down the street. Is that true?"

Me, "Yes ma'am. I was trying to get pictures since it was sitting over the house."

Aunt Dot, "Now you know people say strange stuff happens to you, you know that!"

Me, "Yes ma'am, but a lot of people saw this thing. They say it was sitting over the house, and it was. I don't believe it was after me I just believe it was sitting there."

Aunt Dot took a deep breath, shook her head, and smiled. I reached for the Kool-Aid, and she grabbed my hand, smiling she said:

Aunt Dot, "Boy, you can eat. And I don't know what that thing was, but I want you to promise me if it ever shows up again, you will not follow it, and you will not let it follow you. We don't know what it was; it scared the mess outa of Bryce. He came running through my house like he was crazy! He ran into the back room and slammed the door! I told that boy about running into my house like that. What's wrong with him? He said Ant was in the street, and something was following him and was going to get him! I said get him how? And he said, I don't know, but it's flying over his head and he was just standing there like nothing's happening! So, when I get to the door, and I see this thing over you (she sat back and took a long, deep breath), I don't know what to think. All I can think is that if that thing takes you away from here, Iretha, Aint Lo and Pop, they are going to have a fit! Don't do that again, okay?"

Me, "Okay, I still don't think it was after me. After all, all the books and stories and reports I have read, they only took white people, so I'm good!"

Aunt Dot, "Ant, black people don't write books about this stuff. All it's going to do is bring white people into our neighborhood looking for stuff that we can't find, and they will start taking stuff. And you know that's true. So, you understand; don't fall for these things, right?"

Me, "Yes ma'am, I understand."

Aunt Dot, "You want more food?"

Me, "Yes ma'am, can I please have another piece of ham??"

Aunt Dot, "Yes, you can take what is left. There is ½ piece left. Take it home and share it with the rest. Don't eat the whole thing by yourself, and I know you can."

And just so everybody knows I did eat the whole thing by myself, Yum.

My sister Roz thought that this was hilarious. I am seeing little green men. She just would not accept the fact that it was an object that I saw. I can't say that it was extraterrestrial because I don't know that. Our government, along with other governments, are always experimenting with something. I did not think that it was from our government, but I didn't know what other governments might have developed. I just know that this thing was big, bright, and gone in seconds.

Sunday, December 26, 1976, time 3 PM.

When Sunday dinner was over, my sister and everyone else went to do whatever they needed to do. I heard Shep barking. I looked out the window from my mom's house, and I saw Shep barking at the fence. I thought to myself, 'There goes that stupid dog again with an insane barking, then it hit me: insane barking equals craft in the area. My sister was in her room. I went back to the door, and I said:

Me, "You want to see some little green men? That thing is outside."

Roz, "Where? You saw it again?"

Me, "Oh, so now you're interested? No, I didn't say so, but Shep is barking like crazy again, and that means he sees it! Come with me, let's see!"

She put on her shoes, and we went outside. The dog was barking, looking into the sky. We looked around for a minute, and then we saw it. It was further away, but that's it! It was metallic, reflecting sunlight, and it was sitting still.

Me, "Ha, now what you got to say? Now, who's seeing little green men?"

Roz was just staring. She didn't say a word, she just stared. She turned and went back into the house. I went back to her room,

Me, "You saw it didn't you?"

Roz, "I don't know what that is."

Me, "You think it got little green men in it?"

Roz, "I don't know. What do you think it wants?"

Me, "I don't know as long as it's not me."

Since then, I have never had another encounter like that. I have seen things, but nothing has approached me. The reason I have this entry here is because of my theory. My theory is that these crafts contain demons. These demons need these crafts in order to enter into this dimension. You see, my theory goes like this:

These creatures got put out of Earth's realm as part of the great flood and the placing of the rainbow and God's promise that he would not destroy the Earth for the sake of man again. These creatures were allowed to be on the earth side-by-side with mankind before the flood. During this time, these creatures managed to corrupt men to the point where the only way to fix this was to start over, and that's what God did. These creatures corrupted the very ground, the air, and the sea around them. This is why God had to start over. Mankind was given the strength to overcome them, but they did not; they fell in lockstep with them, and therefore, their fate was similar to theirs.

As Noah and his family left, the earth was cleansed. For those who do not know the number of cleansings, it is 40. Trust and believe when the Lord uses the number 40, something gotta go. It's clean-up time. These creatures, demons, were kicked out of the earth back into whatever realm they came from. I believe the rainbow locks them out. That's our sign and promise from God that they cannot freely roam among us anymore. These vessels are what they use to transgress into our realm.

It is not surprising that they developed this technology. I believe using this technology allows them to stay a little while before they have to go back. I have no way to elaborate, but that is what I believe.

On that day, I witnessed the appearance and disappearance of a craft of unknown technology. After speaking with many others who have similar beliefs about these creatures, I believe that one of the crafts arrived over top of my house. I don't know what it intended to do, but I do believe it was a spying mission. I also believe that the craft was real, but it wasn't really here the whole time. Let me explain.

It seems to me that these crafts enter our atmosphere, our world, zip around for a little while, and then leave. I don't think they have the energy to sustain being in this realm for a prolonged period of time. The energy they use is so great that it limits their time here. As I reviewed what I saw that night, it reminded me of watching a tube television turn-off.

That little white speck of light that appears when you turn off a tube TV. We don't see them now. We saw them on the television sets that weren't digital. That light shrunk away from us at such a volume that it looked as if it was moving very fast. I believe that when this object decided to leave, it was in a window. That we were looking into their dimension. So, it wasn't fully in our dimension. If it had been so, it could not have moved like it did.

Also, the lack of sound tells me it wasn't fully over here. We were looking into a window that gave the appearance of being here, but it was not. It's not an optical illusion because it is real. However, it was looking into a dimensional window that gives us a vision that it's here, but it's not. I believe there are cases where it fully comes over and is on this side when it is experimenting with whatever these creatures do. So, when I saw it zip away, it didn't zip away. That dimensional door closed and gave the appearance of zipping away. The laws of physics cannot be denied, but the laws of interdimensional travel cannot be denied either. The problem here is that we understand some of our laws of physics and how they are applied to motion, but we have no idea as to how in-dimensional travel is even possible. Yet, we have experiences where we do get involved in interdimensional travel. I will get into that in a later event where I traveled through our dimension and saw a person who saw me in their house and met me the next day. In Book 2 people. Be ye prepared.

Getting back to the craft, I asked the question. Was it spying on me? Gathering Intel? This could be the case, but we really don't know. What I do know is that because of the way God has interacted with me, it could be concerning for demons to find out what is going on between God and this person. Just like other people who God is using to move his purpose forward, it would be in the best interest of Satan and his minions to try to find out what is going on. But if you're stuck in another realm and you have tried to stop this progression and failed, an update would, at some point in time, become mandatory. When I look at how God had moved me during my teenage years, if I were against God, I would most certainly attempt to figure out why is this particular figure being moved and empowered in this way and, somewhere along the line, try to put a stop to it.

Some of the things that the Holy Spirit has revealed to me have been eye-openers. I asked about the cavemen and these ancient skeletons that have been found. Science is trying to show that man was not created by God but was the result of a monkey changing into a different kind of monkey-man. While that on its surface is ridiculous enough, what I was told was that these are clones that scientists keep finding. These are the results of Satan's failed attempted experiments in trying to create his own race of men.

He believes that he could create a better man from a better monkey. The problem with that is that God did not create man from a monkey. Therefore, there are no monkeys that you can select that will allow your experimentation to work. This is why such varied amounts of monkey men are scattered all over the place. You see, when Satan was cast out of heaven and fell to the earth, he had dominion over the earth. Seeing as this is jealousy, he decided that God's greatest creation is his beloved mankind and that he could create his own mankind. The biggest problem with this idea for Satan is that he does not have the ability to create life as God does. He can grow some flowers, plants, potatoes, and even a tree, but those things are because God called them into creation, so in essence, there is nothing new to create. Mankind may make a discovery, but the creator has already put the creations in place.

So, in creating these monkey men, it was an unsuccessful attempt to create a man of his own. And now their carcasses litter the landscape. When man fell and was put out of the garden onto the earth, he was given dominion over the earth and it was never taken away. Mankind still has dominion over the earth; this cannot be moved. Nothing that the Lord gives to anyone can be taken away by anyone, including Satan. What he wants to do is to trick you into believing that you don't have dominion. Therefore, he can assume you're right of dominion. This assumption of dominion is impossible because the Lord also always has dominion over all. Hence, the statement of taking back what the devil stole from you is not real. You cannot steal the un-stealable. As the Lord said, "No one can pluck you from my hand." This is standard Scripture.

26 And God said, Let us make man in our image, after our likeness: and let them have dominion over the fish of the sea, and over the fowl of the air, and over the cattle, and over all the earth, and over every creeping thing that creepeth upon the earth. Genesis 1

Now, when Jesus says that Satan is the Lord of this world, what he is saying is that because mankind has not taken up his rightful position, dominion, and authority. Satan has taken that place, but that place is not real. In order for mankind to maintain the legacy that the Lord has given him, they must worship the Lord. In failing to worship properly, he has handed over his right to who will come along and that whoever is Satan.

But as Jesus said, confront him, and he will flee from you. This is because you have been given the authority, dominion, and power to do these things in Jesus' name, Amen.

The question that comes to mind is, if they are following you, are they still continuing to follow you? The answer is yes, they are. As to what end, I don't know. But I do know that as I have walked the warrior's walk, I have encountered them many times, even until an event that happened in June 2014.

Me and my wife were watching television. A thunderstorm had just come through, so it knocked out the satellite. So, as we waited for the satellite to come back, there was a transmission on the television satellite that was not on, but all of a sudden, the TV started to transmit data, and it cleared up, and what we saw we couldn't explain we could only tell you that something was on the screen watching us.

This thing looked like one of those gray aliens that they talked about. I have never seen one before in my life, so the things that I have seen are what people report on TV. It had a wider head than the grays that they showed on TV, but the eyes were the same. The color wasn't gray. It was kind of grayish blue with a red tint to it. His neck was long and narrow with broad shoulders and it seemed to be messing with some instruments in front of it. It did not notice us at first.

It wasn't until I looked over at my wife and said, "Do you see that?" And she turned to me and said (angrily), "Yes. What is that?" I said, "I have no idea. I'm trying to change the channel, but it won't move." We watched this thing for about 60 seconds before it realized we could see it. Once it looked up and looked at us and knew we could see it, it was startled. It started pressing buttons or whatever was in front of it frantically. It was clearly panicking and then the transmission flashed, and it went away. We discussed this as best we could about what had just happened. Was that the satellite messing up? Some excerpt from a movie? We finally had to admit that that looked like one of those great alien creatures looking at us.

I searched the Internet. I asked neighbors and friends. I even called tech support for the satellite people to find out if they had transmitted such a thing. On all channels I checked, there was a no. We have never heard of such a thing. To this day, it still disturbs me that whatever that was could be transmitting in and watching us. Remember, I said disturbs, not surprises.

Monday, December 27, 1976

I was sitting in our living room when I noticed two large black vehicles go across the train track. Were these the infamous men in black coming to work the area? I laughed to myself because I didn't believe the men in black thing either. I continued to watch TV, waiting for the gym to open. Now the fact that the gym was officially closed meant that I had to wait for it to open because we were going to get in and play some basketball. As to how we get in, well that's a different story. But once we got in, I went down with the rest of the guys so we could play some ball. When I got there, two guys told me that there were men in two black cars, asking questions about who saw something strange this past weekend. One of the guys, Leon, said to me, "I didn't tell him nothing about you. You know we know better than that." One of the other guys, Walter told me, "You know they were looking for you. That's why they were asking questions. But we know what to do with this."

I thanked them because I didn't know what else to do. This thing had really gotten creepy, and I still have to say I don't know if it was after me or not, but I do know this. We weren't going to do anything that would bring the white man into our neighborhood looking for anything.

Entry #10: You Are Mine

When you consider everything that happened, you would think that a person would have a better understanding of how God works. Needless to say, this is absolutely not the case. As humans, we deal with many spiritual interactions throughout each day. We don't recognize Most of these when they happen. This is noted in the Scripture when it says:

Hebrews 13:1-2

King James Version

13 Let brotherly love continue.

2 Be not forgetful to entertain strangers: for thereby some have entertained angels unawares.

I can say for myself that I have met angels and initially did not know it was an angel. For you see,

187

part of Satan's plan to deceive us is to get us to believe in something that is not real. That something is these visages of angels with wings flying all over the place, healing, guiding, helping, and so forth with humanity. Now, the truth is angels do help with humanity. Angels are ministering spirits who assist, guide, and help us through our daily lives.

As it is described in Job, we have a hedge that surrounds us, and that hedge is guarded by angels, as noted in the Scripture:

Hebrews 1:13-14

King James Version

13 But to which of the angels said he at any time, Sit on my right hand, until I make thine enemies thy footstool?

14 Are they not all ministering spirits, sent forth

to minister for them who shall be heirs of salvation?

And

Psalm 91:11

King James Version

11 For he shall give his angels charge over thee, to keep thee in all thy ways.

There are many other scriptures that assure us of God's protection. For me, these are my favorites, but everyone gets to pick what they want. For this writing, I am not going to describe every interaction I've had with angels, for there have been hundreds. I can say that each time there was an interaction, there was no halo, no wings, no angelic course (although there were three angels that sang before my first demonic encounter, that story is for book

2), and no glowing clouds. In each case, they helped me deal with some area of my life, and I thank the Lord for that.

After hearing so many stories, my wife (Deborah) asked, "When did these things (demonic encounters) start to happen?"

I answered, "It started at birth because I remember being escorted to my arrival here on earth."

Deborah said, "No, not that. When did it escalate to having to deal with spirits and angels and demons face-to-face?"

I was curious as to why she asked this, so I asked her to explain. She explained that, according to her understanding, before the more advanced type of spiritual interactions would happen, you would need to be empowered by the Holy Spirit. I found it incredulous that I had never thought of that. She was correct. Without the protection and guidance of the Holy Spirit, these interactions would destroy you. This is one of the reasons why Jesus did not allow the disciples to challenge spirits before the arrival of the Holy Spirit. We would get eaten alive, and I nearly did during my first demonic encounter (this entry is in the second book, and it is intense; be prepared). She asked me to remember when the Holy Spirit descended on me, and that would've been when I was 19.

I remember having no idea what was happening at the time. It was one of the most bizarre experiences I had ever had, and it is still that way. That is where entry #10 takes place.

Easter weekend 1981

Location: Greater Mount Sinai Baptist Church, Charlotte, NC

Pastor: Rev. George Cook Junior

It was Easter, and as a family, we attended church. For me, I normally would have gone to church with my mom at Torrance Chapel AME located in Cornelius, North Carolina, but by now, I had found pastor Cook, who gave spirit-filled sermons. There was always a lesson in his sermons, and he rarely "hooped" during service. This was good for me because I felt that church had way too many distractions and not enough focus on the word of God for me. But the good thing about the church is that if you attend, eventually, you will find something that you like enough to stay. It always amazes me when I hear people say the church is full of gossip, rumor, fake, and so on. I often ask what did you expect to be there? This is where people come to get saved. They are not saved on the way in but on the way out.

I was there with my stepmom and my two brothers, Travon and Daymond. In all honesty, I was there because my brothers asked me to go with them this Easter so that we could continue playing Dungeons & Dragons when the church was over. It sounded like a good idea to me, and it was, but I had no idea how this was going to change my life forever.

Rev. Cook had started the sermon, and I don't remember what the sermon was about, but I do remember what happened during the service. Travon was sitting beside me, and Daymond was sitting beside him. I was sitting on the aisle seat while my stepmom sat further in. As Rev. Cook continued to preach, I noticed an unusual but calm feeling around me. At first, I tried to shake it off. I remember thinking it was getting hot, but it didn't feel like heat. Travon noticed me fidgeting and asked me if I was okay. I said yes, I'm good. It is just hot in here. He said I'm cold. They need to turn the air down.

Me, "With all these people in here, we would burn!"

Tray, "Poof, just like a fireball spell!"

We laughed. The usher bumped me on the shoulder. She gave me a look and said, "Too old for that." then she laughed because she heard us. During this time, that feeling of warmth did not leave me. It started to increase. I started looking around to see if anyone else felt this warmth, and I started to become concerned that it was just happening to me. I asked Tray if he felt anything, but he didn't, and he asked me again if I was okay, and I answered yes, but I wasn't.

I noticed the usher started fanning me, so I looked at her and said thanks.

Usher, "You're sweating. Are you okay?"

Me, "Yes, it's just hot in here."

Usher, "Honey, it's freezing in here."

Me, "I know they keep telling me that."

I took a deep breath, and I said to myself, "I got to shake this feeling. I need to concentrate." As I tried to concentrate, the warmth began to take on a new sensation. It had a power! And authority and a presence that was overwhelming to such a degree that there are no words for it. It enveloped me, and it was speaking. I tried to shake it off, but there was no way. I couldn't get it off me. I noticed that I was rocking back and forth. I realized I was speaking, but I could not hear my own speech. I could tell more people had come over to assist me. I remember trying to get up, but there were hands on me, trying to keep me still.

The presence that was causing all this felt like powerful bliss. It felt so good, so wonderful, that at one point, I just released the resistance, and I can tell you I felt like I could split the planet in half with one single stomp of my foot. This was awesome! For one person to have this kind of power is unbelievable! And the only words that I could make out of the many words that were being spoken was, "You are mine. You belong to me. I am with you always. You are mine!" As this presence spoke to me, I repeated it back over and over again. I don't know how long this went on, but I do remember the presence left me a changed person. When I opened my eyes, there were four people, ushers, standing around me, holding me down. The church was singing.

I fell forward, and one of the ushers caught me and held me up. My shirt was wet, and I didn't know where I was initially. It took me a minute to get my bearings back. The usher who kept me from falling forward kept saying, "You're okay, you're okay, amen! You're a big boy! Strong, but it's okay." I'm still wondering what he is talking about. I was weak. My whole body was weak and tired.

I looked around at these ushers who were now fanning themselves. My stepmom was very excited. She grabbed me by the arm and said, "Ant, are you okay? I know what that was, but I don't think I ever saw it like that! The Lord! He had you going! Oh my goodness! They couldn't hold you still. You were trying to run, and the ushers were trying to hold you but couldn't! Travon had to help them."

Me, "Who had me going?"

Stepmom, "Who? The Holy Spirit! You don't remember? Looord, he don't remember. He don't know what just happened!"

Tray, "Ant you don't remember what just happened?"

Me, "What happened to who? Me? I just zoned out, I think. It was that... What was that? Man! I could tear this world in half!"

It was at this point that I realized something had happened, and people were listening to me, so I stopped talking. People started applauding. Pastor Cook said, "Now that is the authority of the hand of God, amen lights!"

198

Service continued. I'm not sure how long services were disrupted, but it did continue. My strength is gone. I was so tired. My brother Daymond did not understand. But he was only 11 at the time. Daymond was trying to stop the ushers because he thought they were attacking me. Travon was excited. He kept saying, "Ant, you were moving, and they were trying to hold you still and they couldn't. And you were talking, but nobody could understand what you were saying. I Heard people saying he is speaking in tongues, and they were trying to listen and hear what you were saying, and nobody could figure it out, and you kept trying to get up, and they kept trying to hold you down, and it looked like you will gonna explode because you folded your arms like this (crossed both fists on my chest) and everybody backed up, and then you just looked up and said something and like you just passed out!"

My stepmom explained it this way, "I saw you and Tray sitting over there playing, and I was going to smack both of you. I saw the usher say something to you because you and Tray were being silly. Then I heard Daymond say, "Something is wrong with Ant." And Lord! You had started twisting and rocking and talking! Another usher came over and tried to fan you and hold you still and she almost fell. Then you stomped your foot, and Lord, it sounded like thunder had gone through the church! Everybody turned, and that's when two of the male ushers ran over to help! Boy, you got to moving! You tried to get up and started talking. Day thought they were attacking you, so I had to grab him to keep him from attacking them! Tray was helping to try to keep you still! Lord! I have seen the Holy Spirit grab some people before, but I ain't never seen nothing like this!"

First, let me confess some things. I had no idea this was coming. I was doing what we always do in church, and that was to watch the clock until it ends. I was 19, and not there yet, spiritually, to understand that God has a serious goal in mind and that we all must have the tools to complete that goal. I did not know that God was empowering me to be able to do his work. I would've thought (age 19 thinking) that God would just tell you what to do, and you do it. Logically, that would make no sense. If God wanted you to dig a ditch, he would prepare a shovel for you to use. Therefore, if God is preparing you to be a warrior, then he will need to prepare your weapons and armor. When you're young, these are things you just don't realize, and when the older people try to tell you this, you just think, well, that's the way he did you. He's not going to do it for me that way. Here is where the old and the young need to have a meeting of the minds.

God is the same today as he was yesterday and as he will be tomorrow. He is the only time traveler in existence. He is the all-powerful, omnipotent Lord of all. There is no other, and there never has been another. So, just remember when he empowers you, and he will empower you, there are things that need to be done on his behalf. Don't say, "Lord, use me!" And expect it not to happen because it will. He does not change his ways for anyone, ever!

Since the Holy Spirit empowered me on that day, I have faced demons, witches, warlocks, wandering spirits, and so on and so forth. My journey continues, and now, at 60+, I still don't understand, but I do embrace it. The wonders that I have encountered in my walk with the Lord are simply astounding!

As we end Book One, I would like to say that so far, it is so good. I have experienced people being raised from the dead. People have been sent to me with requests for healing, but I am no healer. Yet, they said the Lord sent them to me to pray for their healing. I always remind people of this that Jesus said, "It is your faith that made you whole." So, for those who were healed after we prayed together, know that it was your faith and the Lord that healed you. I just did as you asked and prayed for you.

In closing, I would like to thank the Most High Lord, His son Jesus, and the Holy Spirit for guiding me through Book One: Journal of a Christian Warrior. These are things to expect in book Two, where there will be 13 stories chosen from my young adulthood:

Miracle healings

Raise dead

Demonic encounters

Spirit walks

Angelic intervention

Spiritual Possessions

Now that I am empowered and the Holy Spirit dwells within me, as he does with every believer, he empowers us all so be ready and be prepared.

Now, I say a prayer for all who have read to the end of this manuscript.

May the Lord of Host guide you and keep you covered, as well as surround you and shelter you at all times. Please remember that during troubled times when you need to call out, practice calling out unto the Lord before the need is necessary. For the wiles of the devil surround us. We are in the world, but we are not of the world. Remember, we fight a spiritual foe. Your guns will do you no good. You cannot run, and you cannot hide, and no walls will protect you. Your weapon is your faith, and your protection is your heavenly father. Call him in trouble times. Practice a psalm where you call to him and not a song where you curse and call to that. There will come a time when you will have to make that call and make sure that you don't stumble and say the wrong thing and have the wrong thing happen.

Now to he who is able to keep us from falling, ask for blessings in all that you do in Jesus' name; I pray, Amen.

www.ingramcontent.com/pod-product-compliance
Lightning Source LLC
LaVergne TN
LVHW091252080426
835510LV00007B/231